READING THE FORESTED LANDSCAPE

A Natural History of New England

READING THE FORESTED LANDSCAPE

A Natural History of New England

TOM WESSELS

Etchings and Illustrations by Brian D. Cohen

Foreword by Ann H. Zwinger

The Countryman Press ~ Woodstock, Vermont

Library of Congress Cataloging-in-Publication Data

Wessels, Tom. 1951–
Reading the forested landscape : a natural history of New England / Tom Wessels ; etchings and illustrations by Brian D. Cohen ; foreword by Ann Zwinger. — 1st pbk. ed.
p.   cm.
Includes bibliographical references and index.
ISBN 0-88150-420-3 (pbk. : alk. paper)
1. Forest ecology—New England. 2. Landscape ecology—New England. 3. Forest dynamics—New England. 4. Forest ecology. 5. Landscape ecology. 6. Forest dynamics. I. Title.
[QK121.W47 1998]
577.3'0974—dc21   98-13140
                                                                               CIP

The text of this book is composed in Bembo and Gill Sans. Cover and text design by Angie Hurlbut. Hand-colored etching by Brian D. Cohen. Map composed by Karen Savary, copyright © 1997 The Countryman Press.

Published by The Countryman Press, PO Box 748, Woodstock, Vermont 05091

Distributed by W. W. Norton & Company, Inc., 500 Fifth Avenue, New York, New York 10110

Printed in The United States of America

10 9 8 7 6 5 4 3

To Marcia, whose ecological eye is as sharp as a hawk's

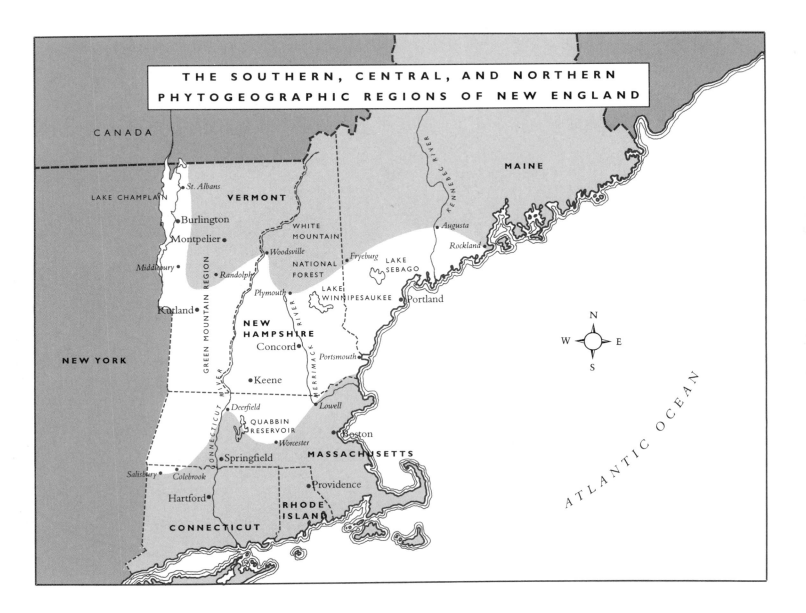

THE SOUTHERN, CENTRAL, AND NORTHERN
PHYTOGEOGRAPHIC REGIONS OF NEW ENGLAND

TABLE OF CONTENTS

ACKNOWLEDGMENTS

I am grateful to all those who helped to make this book a reality. I thank my colleagues in the Environmental Studies Department at Antioch New England Graduate School for picking up the slack during my sabbatical. To be able to work on a manuscript and know that things were well in hand was a real gift. Marcia and Kelsey, thanks for being so patient with my quirky writing habits and for not tempting me to go out and play. Thanks to Richard Thompson and Chard DeNoird for their early and ever-present encouragement, and to Dog Breslaw for his candid comments and guidance on writing style. Thanks also to Peggy Robinson for her efforts in moving this project along. Mitch Thomashow was critical in helping me to brainstorm the book's problem-solving approach by telling me to write the book the way I teach my classes—such a simple but profound suggestion.

I am indebted to Helen Whybrow at The Countryman Press, whose long-term interest, support, and fine attention to detail ushered this book not only to publication, but also to such a handsome outcome. I also wholeheartedly thank Ann Zwinger for her encouragement and gracious support.

I could not have written this book without the close supervision of Chip Blake of *Orion* magazine and Sabine Hrechdakian of *Terra Nova* magazine. As skilled editors and former students of my plant communities course at Antioch, Chip and Sabine not only helped mold the book, but they also taught me how to write. Whatever quality of writing is found in the following pages, it is the direct result of Chip and Sabine's extensive efforts on my behalf.

Finally, my deepest gratitude to my good friend and former Putney School colleague, Brian D. Cohen, for his superb etchings and illustrations. Brian's work was essential in creating this book's unique style, and the collaboration we developed to meld the text and etchings was such fun.

FOREWORD

I agree with Tom Wessels that we tend to "teach nature" in unrelated segments, a collection of nice facts that look like an unworked jigsaw puzzle spread out all over the table, pieces unconnected and, for the time, meaningless. If we know the names of our neighbors and the streets in our neighborhood, why don't we also know our natural neighborhood, who and what lives there and why, who eats whom, who nurtures whom, who passes through and who remains, who's native and who's interloper? To this end, Wessels proposes a broader look at the landscapes around us, the bigger questions that bring true understanding and true appreciation of our home place, of the place we live.

To give us this understanding, he takes an ecosystem dear to his heart, the forests of central New England, and walks us through, touching bough and bole, enlivening and interpreting all those very obvious features that we somehow seem to miss because we haven't learned to look or to think about the natural world as a well-woven whole.

The factual information in *Reading the Forested Landscape* is superb and what we as observers dearly need. But Wessels goes beyond, to link and knot and tie, to weave and wonder all those lovely facts together in a coherent tapestry of greens and browns and birdsong and mushroom stalk.

This book invites slow and luxurious reading, the rewards of knowing a landscape well—and if not New England forests, then the southwestern desert or the midwestern prairie: The principles are the same. But most of all this is a story of home, often fascinating, sometimes familiar, occasionally surprising, the place we know so well but know so little about.

Ann H. Zwinger

INTRODUCTION

In 1954, when I was three, my family moved from the industrial shores of Lake Erie to the suburban shores of Long Island Sound. We settled into a housing development typical of those built just after World War II. Evenly spaced, half-acre lots followed tree-lined streets named after the war's heroes: MacArthur Drive, Nimitz Place, Eisenhower Street. It was this last high-ranking road that separated our yard from a woodland roughly seventy acres in size. "The woods," as we kids called it, was a wilderness that pulled me daily into its embrace until the age of twelve, when it, too, was subdivided into half-acre lots. Like most neighborhood boys, I climbed trees, built forts, played cowboys and Indians, and scampered up cliffs, but the woods was more than a mere playground. I spent nearly every day exploring its silty streams, skunk cabbage–covered swamps, and numerous ledges until I knew those seventy acres as if they were my home.

It is amazing just how sharp childhood memories can be. Even now, from my boyhood memories alone, I can picture that woodland clearly enough to create a decent map of the area. Although as a child I did not know the names of trees, I can recall the woods' various species by their bark textures. Only later, when taking dendrology at the University of New Hampshire, did I learn that the elegantly straight-boled trees in which we built our forts were called yellow poplar and that the large, shaggy-barked trees of the skunk cabbage lowlands were red maples. Without a conscious effort, and simply through my sensory experience of the woods, I learned to perceive changes in forest composition.

As an adult I have taken this process a step further. Now when I observe a change in forest composition, I work to understand why it has occurred. My memory of "the woods" enables me not only to mentally map its different forests, but also—now, looking back—to understand the origin and history of those forests. In short, even though separated by time, I can *read* the landscape of my childhood woods.

The idea of "reading the landscape" was first described by May Watts in her 1964 book of the same title. This was an influential work for me as a college undergraduate because it was my first exposure to the natural history of landscapes as opposed to the natural history of individual organisms. Yet I didn't really learn the process of reading the landscape until I became a graduate student at the University of Colorado. At that time I worked under the tutelage of plant ecologist Dr. John W. Marr. It was Marr who took me into the ponderosa pine–covered foothills of Colorado's Front Range and asked me to explain *why* two contiguous forests were different in their composition. This process was repeated many times in my studies with Marr, and I quickly developed a new way of seeing landscapes—one that focused on their history. But Marr taught me more than the process of how to read forests. He was a rare ecologist who stressed the importance of having a strong emotional connection to landscapes alongside an analytical one. The very foundation of this book and my twenty years of teaching lies with John Marr.

Through Marr, plant identification became a language, one that I could apply to reading the story of a landscape the way I apply English to the reading of a book. To make that analogy even stronger, the book should be *The Adventures of Sherlock Holmes,* by Sir Arthur Conan Doyle. The choice of literary genre is relevant because reading the landscape is a process similar to solving mysteries.

I now live in southeastern Vermont, where my favorite pastime is to wander through the fields and forests that surround my home. Whenever I encounter a change in the composition of the forest, such as a dense stand of hemlock abutting an older stand of beech and sugar maple, I am compelled to solve the mystery: What created this change in vegetation? Until I have done so, I'll comb the site, looking for clues that relate to the history of each stand. To people not as experienced in the process of "reading the landscape," I might appear somewhat like Holmes through Watson's eyes. Yet this process is not as difficult as it seems. It demands only some new observational skills—and knowledge about the kinds of clues to look for.

Reading the Forested Landscape is a guide to deciphering the varied forest patterns of central New England. It introduces the reader to the clues that can explain changes in forest composition. In the majority of cases, these changes will be the result of differing forest *disturbance histories*—the impact of past logging, fires, or blowdowns on a forest. The book also describes the dramatic changes, of both climatic and human origin, that have taken place in central New England's landscape during the past several thousand years. Each chapter focuses on a single form of disturbance that has had a significant impact on the forests of this region, including: abandonment of pastureland, fire, beaver activity, blowdowns, forest blights, and logging. The chapters follow a chronology, beginning with disturbances that were more prominent in the past. Thus, each chapter accomplishes two things. The first is helping people read the history written in the landscape by seeking clues that explain differences in forest composition. The second is giving a historical context to each form of disturbance; for example, the return of forest following abandoned pastureland was most common in the later half of the nineteenth century. The history of each form of disturbance is covered in the second part of every chapter, under the heading "A Look Back."

In keeping with the idea of solving mysteries, every chapter is preceded by one of Brian Cohen's elegant etchings. Each etching depicts a landscape that displays evidence of a single form of disturbance. Some of the etchings are rendered after actual forest sites; others are idealized composites of several sites that allow all the evidence of a particular disturbance to be presented in a single landscape view. The etchings are not meant to be exact representations of our regional forests; they are stylized to highlight the evidence of disturbance, so certain forest components such as understory vegetation are often missing. In some of the etchings I will be identifying trees or attributes about the site that couldn't otherwise be perceived.

The etching's evidence is then carefully pointed out in the chapter, leaving the most telling clues for last so that you can consider the evidence and develop your own ideas about the disturbance prior to the chapter's end. This way, by reading the book and deciphering the etchings, you will actually develop the skills necessary for "reading the landscape." So as not to give away the solutions, the chapters are cryptically titled.

Central New England is a specific *phytogeographic region*—an area that shares the same climate and is characterized by similar vegetation. Within any such region, only three factors affect the composition of plant communities: topography, substrate, and disturbance history. *Topography* describes the lay of the land, particularly the steepness of its slopes and the directions they face. Topography also involves changes in elevation, but this book only focuses on areas below two thousand feet; above this elevation, climatic conditions and forests become much more similar to those of northern New England. *Substrate,* whether clay, silt, sand, gravel, glacial till, or bedrock, is the mineral material on which soil—a complex mixture of minerals, living organisms, and dead organic material—develops. *Disturbance history* relates to the kinds of disturbances, and the accompanying revegetation, that affect landscapes through time.

Chapters 1 through 6 deal with forest disturbance, focusing on logging, pasture abandonment, fire, beaver activity, blowdowns, and forest blights (though not in that order). Chapter 7 explores the impact of topography and substrate on plant community composition and lists important *eco-indicator species*—plants that grow in very specific locations and whose presence indicates precise attributes of their sites. The final chapter considers the future of central New England's forests.

It is necessary to delve further into the role of disturbance in forests and other ecosystems since it plays such a critical role in the balance of nature, and reading its patterns is the prime focus of this book. Disturbance is a force that counters the successional growth of ecosystems. Together, disturbance and *succession*—the changes in vegetation that follow a disturbance through time—are like the opposing but balancing yin and yang of Taoist thought. Both are important to regional ecosystem health in the sense that if one dominates the other, a region becomes, ecologically speaking, poorer. If we could hypothetically restrict disturbance from central New England, our regional biodiversity would drop dramatically, since countless organisms thrive in sites altered by disturbance. However, if disturbance is too frequent, fragile and older ecosystems, and the species associated with them, are lost. The absence of old-growth forest in our region tells us that human-induced disturbance has been much too frequent in recent centuries.

Even though humans are responsible for widespread ecosystem disturbance, we tend to have a cultural bias against natural disturbances. A headline in a local newspaper a few years ago typified this bias when it stated, *Fifteen Acres Destroyed by Fire*. It sounded, interpreting the headline literally, as if the acreage were gone, swallowed up and replaced by a gaping black hole. But upon visiting the site, I found the land still intact and walked through what was going to be a fine blueberry patch in a couple of years.

Our New England ecosystems have evolved with nature's disturbances—fire, blowdowns, and beavers—through millions of years, but they are just beginning to adjust to recent human alterations in the form of agricultural activity, logging, and introduced forest pathogens. In terms of ecosystem health, we have nothing to fear from nature's disturbances; blowdowns, for example, mix forest soil by uprooting trees to make nutrients more available to the ecosystem. However, it is less clear how the broad-scale, human-induced disturbances of the past few centuries will eventually affect our woodlands since they are, ecologically speaking, new regimes to which our forests have yet to evolve.

I don't mean to imply that people should stop farming or logging; humans have altered the landscapes in which they live for more than one hundred thousand years. Changing our surroundings is in large part what it means to be a human. But as a species, through the last couple of centuries we have dramatically increased both the area and the frequency of our disturbance regime. To give ecosystems the time to adjust, our landscape alterations need to be more cautious and thoughtful.

The "transition forest" is a name that has been applied to the woodlands of central New England. It is an appropriate label because this phytogeographic region is the transition zone between the two great forest biomes of eastern North America, the temperate deciduous forests that extend from Georgia to Massachusetts and the boreal coniferous forests that extend from northern New England into Labrador. Sandwiched between these two expansive biomes is central New England, a mixing ground where more than one hundred species of woody plants find the limits of either their northern or southern ranges. This mingling of species creates a region with a far greater diversity of plants, and plant communities, than any other area in the northeastern United States.

EASTERN RED CEDAR

Because central New England is a transitional zone, it is difficult to pinpoint precise boundaries designating where it begins and ends (see the map in the front of the book). For the purposes of this book I use a few species of trees to delineate these borders. For the southern boundary I have traced a line where the proportion of eastern red cedar to common juniper in old pastures is roughly equal. Once common juniper predominates, we find ourselves in central New England. The change in species is due to decreasing winter temperatures, to which the upright eastern red cedar is less tolerant. To the south of this line, as winter temperatures become warmer, red cedar quickly gains dominance. A drive along any of Connecticut or Rhode Island's highways shows they are often bordered by stands of red cedar and an absence of common juniper.

COMMON JUNIPER

A line where spruce and fir begin to dominate valley bottoms, which collect the cold air that creates short growing seasons, defines the northern boundary. This change also occurs with an increase in elevation. Once above two thousand feet in central New England, we have also traveled into the phytogeographic region of northern New England. In cold climates, with short growing seasons, evergreen conifers are more competitive than broad-leaved deciduous trees. (For readers interested in learning more about the vegetated landscapes of southern and northern New England, I highly recommend Neil Jorgensen's *A Sierra Club Naturalist's Guide to Southern New England* and Peter Marchand's *North Woods*.)

Although this book focuses on the landscapes of central New England, it will be very useful for people living in any forested region of the United States. Many of the forest types and particular species of trees will be different in other phytogeographic regions, but the evidence of disturbance—whether from fire, logging, blowdowns, or beaver activity—will be the same. The process of reading forested landscapes, outlined in this book, can be successfully applied to any North American woodland.

Since 1976, I have taught graduate, undergraduate, high school, and elementary school students the process of reading the landscape; I have seen people forge a stronger connection to their local countryside. It also is a wonderful science activity for students to be engaged in, as the process involves making observations about changes in forest composition, developing hypotheses to explain the observed changes, seeking evidence to support or reject the hypotheses, and reformulating the hypotheses based on the evidence.

Most of my teaching on reading forested landscapes has occurred in my plant communities course at Antioch New England Graduate School. I hear from students who have taken this course that it is a "link between thinking in categories and thinking in terms of connectedness," that "it brings natural history to a much broader scale where forest communities are the focus of identification," and that reading the landscape "led me to a new intimacy with the land that I take with me everywhere." I also have students from the Putney School, an independent secondary school, who tell me that "learning to read the landscape was one of the most engaging skills I developed at Putney," and "I feel at home in forests wherever I go because I see the same patterns." I am convinced that reading the landscape is a process that supports many different aspects of natural history and pulls them together in meaningful ways.

Most people who share a love of nature have been taught to see the landscape in a piecemeal way. They know how to identify plants, birds, amphibians, and fungi. They may even know quite a bit about the ecology of these organisms, but they have not learned to see nature in a larger context. It is wonderful to know nature through one-on-one encounters with other organisms, but it is perhaps more empowering to gain a fuller understanding of the patterns that have shaped its landscapes. Through some knowledge of history and the broader view of seeing a forest and not just its trees, we begin to see the forces that shape a place. This new way of seeing creates reverence, respect, a sense of inclusion, and accountability. Reading the landscape is not just about identifying landscape patterns; more importantly, it is an interactive narrative that involves humans and nature. For those interested in enhancing their sense of place, I know of no better way than by becoming intimately acquainted with their local forests and the fascinating stories they tell. *Reading the Forested Landscape* is a guide to that end.

chapter one

THE AGE DISCONTINUITY

New England is blessed with a diverse array of forests. Whether they are young, dense stands of hemlock or older groves of beech and maple, each has a specific story to tell about its origins and development. Sometimes these stories are difficult to read; through time, nature's editing becomes bolder, and important parts of the tale are lost. In other forests, like the one depicted in the preceding etching, the stories remain intact and are easy to follow, once you have learned how to read forested landscapes. To develop this ability, you need to observe forests in new ways, paying particular attention to patterns of *forest structure,* the spacing and sizes of trees, and *forest composition,* the species of trees present. By the end of this book, you may be surprised by your new understanding of forested landscapes.

Let's begin by examining the forest in this first etching. What is most striking to you about its structure? There are some very large trees in this stand. The tree in the center is a red oak about three feet in diameter. At this size it is probably more than a hundred years of age. Small trees are also present, such as the triple-trunked red maple directly to the right of the oak and the majority of the trees that fill the background.

But medium-sized trees are missing. This is called an *age discontinuity*—a somewhat formal term for a forest that is missing trees of a certain age group. In this case it is the medium-sized trees that are poorly represented. Only two conditions can create an age discontinuity: the growth and development of a young forest or a disturbance to an older forest.

A young forest typically develops a gap in age classes when its canopy first closes. A closed canopy restricts shafts of sunlight from reaching the forest floor, and because the canopy in a young forest is so close to the ground, it creates dense shade that allows little vegetation to grow. It may take a couple of decades, as lower branches die off and the canopy moves skyward, before tree seedlings begin to show their presence. Even though the maturing and elevated canopy allows more light to reach the forest floor, light levels remain low and seedlings grow slowly. As the canopy trees continue their competitive race toward the sun, slower-growing individuals don't have the stamina to keep up. Their death creates gaps. The increased light through the openings allows seedlings to become saplings, which grow into young pole-sized trees. New seedlings continue to invade the woodland, but an age discontinuity between canopy trees and the younger poles standing beneath them becomes clearly visible. It will remain so until large, slower-growing individuals die off, creating big gaps in the canopy that become filled by the faster-growing former poles. It may take a century before the visible evidence of an age discontinuity is erased by younger trees filling the canopy gaps.

Because the largest trees depicted in this scene are probably more than a hundred years old, we can discount forest youth as the cause of the age discontinuity. Instead, we can look to some form of disturbance as being the progenitor of this forest's missing age class. What was the disturbance? Was it logging, fire, a blowdown, or some form of defoliation that removed the middle-aged understory trees?

Further evidence allows us to eliminate some of these possibilities and provides us with clues to solve the mystery. For example, there is a downed tree in this forest. It could be the result of a *blowdown*—a wind event strong enough to uproot and topple live trees. Certain clues make this possibility questionable. If we look closer, the downed tree appears to be more likely the result of *deadfall.* The standing dead snag to the left of the large red oak, you will notice, looks similar to the downed tree, as both are devoid of bark and display the same degree of weathering. Lacking any other evidence of downed trees, it would be a sound conclusion that this tree died before falling. Its roots rotted to the point where they couldn't support the upright trunk, and it fell. We can also throw out the blowdown hypothesis because the trees most susceptible to windthrow are the largest canopy trees, not the more wind-protected, middle-aged, subcanopy trees, and it is the latter that are missing from this landscape.

Possibly the medium-sized trees were killed by defoliating diseases or insects, such as the oak-loving gypsy moth or maple-munching saddled-prominent caterpillar. But there are two problems with this scenario. Although insects and disease organisms discriminate among species of trees, they usually don't discriminate among trees of different sizes. Also, trees stripped of their leaves often die because their roots become starved of carbohydrate energy following defoliation. There is evidence to suggest that whatever removed the middle-sized trees left their root systems intact and alive.

DOWNED TREE

DEAD SNAG

MULTIPLE-TRUNKED TREE

The disturbance left behind trees that grew up to be *coppiced,* a fancy term for trees that have more than one trunk growing from their root system. The red maple to the right of the central oak is a classic example, as is the small double-trunked tree at the far left of the etching. *Multiple trunked* is another, possibly more descriptive, term for trees with this growth form. With the exception of gray birch and speckled alder (species that normally display coppiced growth), the only way for a tree to become multiple trunked is for the trunk to be killed while the root system is left alive. When this happens, the roots quickly respond by throwing up a number of stump-sprouts, a few of which eventually grow to tree size.

So, what could kill the aboveground portion of a tree and leave its root system vital? Both the cutting and the burning of a hardwood's trunk leave an intact root system that can stump-sprout. The cutting and burning of coniferous trees—pines (with the exception of pitch pine, which will be discussed later in this chapter), hemlock, and spruce—kill the root system. Having eliminated the possibility of a blowdown or a defoliation event, we can now consider either logging or fire as the cause of this forest's most recent disturbance.

BASAL SCAR

Basal scars

At the start of this chapter I asked you to identify the most striking aspect of this forest's structure. I should now admit that I was a little disingenuous in my response, for the very first thing I noticed in the etching was not the age discontinuity, but the dramatic scar at the base of the large, central red oak. This *basal scar,* along with another on a big tree behind and to the left of the red oak, supports the idea of disturbance by either logging or fire. However, in order to play the game of elimination by looking for evidence of defoliation or a blowdown as the cause of the age discontinuity, I wanted to delay discussion of these slow-to-heal tree wounds.

Basal scars are created when the tree's bark is removed, either by fire damage or by some form of collision. Trees that line roadways often display triangular-shaped scars received from automobile impacts. In the forest, basal scars not due to fire are either the result of log skidding—the dragging of logs out of the woods—or of a falling tree hitting the base of a neighbor. This is a rare event in forests, as canopy branches either catch falling trees or deflect them away from their bases. The placement of the basal scars is the critical clue in determining whether logging or fire was responsible for their origin.

Suppose a fire burned up a moderately steep, forested hillside. On which side of the trees would most basal scarring occur? This is a question that often confounds my students. The most common response is the downhill side. Intuitively, this seems correct because a fire burning upslope directly confronts this side of the trees. Yet most basal scars are found on the uphill side. How could that be? The answer lies in the presence of *fuel pockets*—dead leaves and sticks that have accumulated at the base of the tree's uphill side due to the pull of gravity, which slowly tugs at forest litter and results in its slow, downslope migration. Any large, upright object, such as a boulder or tree trunk, impedes this flow much as a dam obstructs the flow of a river. When fire reaches a fuel pocket, it burns far longer than it does on the litter-free, downhill side of the tree. And if the fuel pocket is big enough, the fire destroys the tree's bark, creating an uphill basal scar.

When a forest fire occurs on relatively level terrain, the fire scars are random in their placement, occurring wherever fuel, usually in the form of downed limbs, lies close to the base of a tree. The same random pattern is also created by falling trees hitting their neighbors. However, basal scars resulting from skidding do not show a random pattern—they often face one another from the opposite sides of logging roads, giving rise to the term *opposing basal scars*. As logs are dragged through the forest on these roads, they hit the base of trees, removing the bark and providing a clear testament to the forest's logging legacy.

Not only does the etching's central red oak display a basal scar, but also another can be seen in the background, on a tree to the left of the oak. The topography of this landscape is fairly level, so what are we to make of the placement of these scars? On their own, the two basal scars do not provide enough information for us to state with certainty whether it was logging or fire that created them. To decide which disturbance impacted this forest, we need to return to the first observation I made about this forest—its age discontinuity—but this time from the perspective of a logger.

Place yourself in the role of a logger. What kinds of trees would you cut? What kinds of trees would you leave? Many of the large trees in the etching are oaks, highly valued for timber. The majority of the multiple-trunked specimens are red maple, a species of lower timber value. Would a logger remove the smaller, lower-valued trees while leaving the larger, higher-valued trees? Probably not. The age discontinuity depicted in the etching does not support logging, but it does support disturbance by fire. The trees most likely to survive a burn are the largest individuals with the thickest bark, while small and medium-sized trees run a higher risk of death. Following the fire, small multiple-trunked specimens will replace those that were killed, filling

BASAL SCAR

the understory, but an age discontinuity between these smaller trees and the large, surviving, canopy trees will be clearly visible. Having now eliminated forest youth, blowdown, defoliation, and logging, we are left with the conclusion that sometime in its past this forest experienced a fire hot enough to kill a number of trees.

Two more pieces of evidence support this theory. To the left of the central oak is a standing dead snag. Its *whorled limbs*—branches arranged in an encircling pattern—reveal it as a conifer, most likely a white pine. Both white pine and hemlock are the region's most common needle-bearing trees, but hemlock doesn't display distinct limb whorls. The snag's weathered look also suggests it has been dead for some time, yet it does not seem to support any visible fungal growth. The same is true for its downed companion. Trees killed by defoliation or competition for canopy space often develop significant fungal growth within a decade. Yet pines, spruce, and oaks, if killed by fire or lightning, become extremely rot resistant and can remain as fungal-free, standing dead snags for over fifty years. Other species of trees heat-killed by fire decay relatively quickly. Because the snags in the etching are whorled-limbed conifers and highly rot resistant, the best guess is that they were white pines, heat-killed by a very hot fire—along with the red maples, whose original trunks have since rotted away and been replaced by coppiced specimens. Only a hot fire could kill large white pines—trees that have thick, heat-protecting bark.

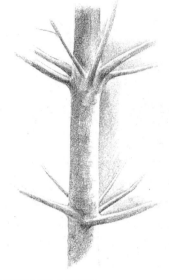

WHORLED LIMBS

Forest composition

Further evidence lending support to the fire theory is the species composition of this forest. Two types of trees in this stand serve as eco-indicators of warm, dry sites in central New England: white oak (the scaly-barked tree at the far right of the etching) and shagbark hickory (toward the far left). Not only do these trees grow in warm, dry sites, but also their barks are adapted to survive hot fires.

The bulk of a tree is simply dead wood. The only living part of a tree, other than its leaves, is a thin layer of tissue just underneath the bark. This layer, only a few millimeters thick, is the cambium. The best way for a tree to protect this cambial tissue from being damaged by fire is to surround it with thick, protective bark. Similarly, we protect ourselves from the cold by putting on layers of clothing to capture the insulating qualities of dead air space. This strategy could also shield us from excess heat. Fire-adapted trees have a comparable strategy, only they use layers of bark in the form of shag or scales. Thin, tight-barked trees like birch, maple, hemlock, and beech are easily heat-killed by a fire. Red oak, which has thicker bark, does somewhat better. But the most fire-adapted hardwood trees in our region are the white oak, chestnut oak, shagbark hickory, and the once common American chestnut.

WHITE OAK

Even more fire-adapted than these hardwood trees are certain species of pine. Large white pines develop a thick layer of bark that has insulating properties slightly better than those of red oak. Red pine has loose, many-layered, flaky bark making it more fire-adapted than white pine. But the most fire-adapted tree in the region is the pitch pine. It has dramatically thick, layered bark and is the only conifer in central New England that can stump-sprout following fire or logging. The trunk of a pitch pine, from the ground up, is covered with needle tufts that surround *adventitious buds*—buds found in unusual places such as on the trunks of trees. Each bud is capable of giving rise to new growth in the event that portions of the tree are killed. If all of a pitch pine's needles are burned off, these buds will allow the tree to refoliate. Such adaptations, along with the ability of pitch pine seeds to aggressively colonize burned areas, make this species of tree the most fire tolerant in central New England.

Stands of pitch pine are found in only two kinds of sites in our region: very well-drained sands and hot, dry, rocky exposures. Both sites are prone to the highest frequency of fires in central New England. Often associated with the pitch pine on these sites is the region's smallest oak, the very fire-tolerant bear oak. Stands of pitch pine and bear oak, in fact, owe their existence to frequent fires. These trees grow slowly, need full sunlight, and require bare soil for their seeds to become established. Frequent fires eliminate the faster-growing species of pines and oaks that would eventually overtop and kill them. They also create exposed soil, which is a perfect seedbed for pitch pine regeneration. If fires are suppressed on these sites, the pitch pine and bear oak will be replaced by white pine and red and white oak.

SHAGBARK HICKORY

The next most fire-prone forests are stands of red pine growing on dry, rocky slopes, which are the only sites in central New England where stands of native red pine are found. All other red-pine forests are plantations, the majority of which were planted between 1930 and 1960 in response to a fungal epidemic that affected white pine (discussed in chapter 4). Following red pine, fires most often affect dry-sited forests, like the one in the etching, composed of white oak and shagbark hickory.

All of these fire-adapted communities share another prominent feature: The ground cover is usually dominated by either lowbush blueberry or, on the warmest sites, black huckleberry. These two species of shrubs thrive in areas with frequent fires, which

CHARCOAL

BLACK FUNGUS

boost their berry-producing capabilities by allowing new branches rich in flower buds to replace older, burned branches. This capability explains why the blueberry barrens of Maine are burned every few years to ensure a good crop. Whenever a forest dominated by either pitch pine, native red pine, white oak, or shagbark hickory, with an understory of blueberry or huckleberry, is encountered in central New England, it is a safe bet that evidence of fire will be close at hand.

Although fire is most common in forests dominated by the above species, it also frequents forests dominated by either white pine, red oak, or beech. All of these species deposit leaf litter that is resistant to decay, and this litter bed greatly restricts herbaceous plant growth. Moist, green plants on the forest floor dramatically dampen fire activity, and forests lacking herbaceous ground cover become fire-prone. As all the tree species listed in this paragraph grow well in dry, warm sites and produce rot-resistant leaf litter, forests dominated by these species are also good places to look for past fire activity.

There remains one bit of evidence of fire that has not yet been discussed: the presence of charcoal. Charcoal is a problematic clue for fire in New England for a couple of reasons. The first is that after a few years it may not be visible. Ground charcoal becomes buried by leaf litter, and charring on trees is uncommon except in blazes hot enough to set living trees on fire. These very hot fires are rare in northeastern forests, where moisture levels in the litter, ground vegetation, and trees keep conflagrations from occurring. Even more problematic than the lack of visible charcoal is the possibility of being misled by a black fungus, a species of *Ascomycetes,* that usually coats the surface of decaying beech and maple. The fungus looks very much like charred wood but is simply part of the normal decay process. Unlike charred wood, whose surface is covered with rectangular blocks of charcoal, the fungal coating is smooth and will not leave black marks on the fingers. Until you learn to identify this fungal species, it is best not to look for charcoal as evidence of fire.

The landscape depicted in this etching has all the signs of a fire-prone ecosystem. It is dominated by oaks and shagbark hickory, displays basal fire scars, has rot-resistant standing dead snags, multiple-trunked fire-sensitive hardwoods, and an age discontinuity in which the middle-aged trees are missing.

Although forest fires are not often encountered in central New England (during the past twenty years, I have witnessed only three active fires), it does not mean that fire is unusual, nor does it mean that it has not played a significant role in shaping the region's landscape. The numerous hilltop fire towers that dot the countryside attest to the frequency of fire. Most of the region's fires burn limited acreages and are quickly extinguished, explaining their lack of visibility. Yet they are far more common than most people realize, particularly on dry slopes with a southern exposure. Logging, blowdowns, and pasturing may have limned our landscape with broad, bold strokes, but fire has left its mark in a more selective, discriminating manner.

A LOOK BACK

Today, more than 95 percent of the wildfires in central New England are the unintentional result of human activity. The rest are caused by lightning strikes. This is a dramatic change from precolonial times, when the majority of forest fires were intentionally set by Native people. Although the frequency of fire in the region is probably greater today, the acreage involved is far less than it was four hundred years ago. Whereas local fire companies mobilize to extinguish forest blazes, Native people encouraged their spread.

Fire was the first landscape management tool used by humans. Archaeological research suggests that our hominid ancestors may have controlled fire half a million years ago. Certainly by the time people migrated from Asia to North America, during the latter part of the last glaciation, fire was well established as a management tool. The extent and distribution of ground charcoal from recent archaeological digs in the Kampoosa Bog of Stockbridge, Massachusetts, suggest intentional understory burning by Native peoples as much as five thousand years ago.

When the first explorers and settlers ventured from Europe to New England, Native American use of fire was well at hand, especially around the coastal regions of southern and central New England, where Native populations were highest. Thomas Morton, who explored the coastal regions of Massachusetts, New Hampshire, and Maine, wrote in his 1632 book, *New English Canaan,* "The Salvages are accustomed, to set fire in the Country, in all places where they come; and to burne it, twize a yeare, vixe at the Springe, and the fall of the leafe. The reason that mooves them to doe so, is because it would other wise be so overgrowne with underweeds, that it would be all a copice wood, and the people would not be able to passe through the Country out of a beaten path."

Natives had a variety of reasons for managing forests with fire other than just keeping them passable. Burning the forest litter was a way of controlling mosquito and blackfly populations, because adults of these species seek refuge under fallen leaves. Burning understory vegetation also made it possible to hunt with bow and arrow. Today's bow hunters often have to clear an alley through the forest vegetation to get a clear shot.

The removal of litter also made it possible to stalk game quietly. As a young boy, enamored of Indians and growing up in Connecticut, I remember trying to walk silently through oak forests in moccasined feet, but I was never successful. Cracking sticks and the rustle of dry leaves made silent movement impossible. It wasn't until college that I learned of the historic use of fire by Native Americans—and realized why my childhood attempts had failed. A litter-free forest floor covered in grasses and legumes would have made the task so much easier.

Natives of southern New England were permaculturalists, and created forest ecosystems that were highly productive in food. Fire was used to increase and maintain berry-producing plants, most notably blueberries and huckleberries. Over time, burning also selected for fire-tolerant, nut-producing trees, such as American chestnut, white oak, and shagbark hickory. The most fire tolerant of the region's hardwood trees also produce the most edible nuts, and it's no accident that they were the dominant overstory species in New England forests managed by fire.

Large crops of nuts and berries were important food sources for wildlife too, and their abundance sustained large populations of game. Because fire removed leaf litter and increased sunlight by eliminating subcanopy trees, forest floors were covered with grasses and other herbaceous plants that provided good forage for grazing animals.

Protective cover and woody browse were found either in lowlands too wet to burn or in areas where the more common ground fires had grown into wildfires that consumed not only litter and small trees but also much of the forest. These hot fires occurred in woods that either were not regularly burned or had abundant ground fuel due to windthrow. The young, dense forests that grew up on these sites stood out in sharp contrast to the open-understory forests maintained by regular ground fires.

The result was a mosaic of old-growth forests, some maintained by ground fires and dominated by large chestnut, oak, and hickory. These were bisected by unburned areas, mostly in wet lowlands, and forest in different successional stages generated either by much hotter burns or by blowdowns. Because of its ample forage, this forest mosaic supported greater densities of game species such as deer, bear, squirrel, turkey, and grouse than any forested region found in New England today.

These precolonial, fire-managed woodlands looked dramatically different from New England's present forests. They were parklike, with massive hardwoods creating a canopy over forest floors carpeted with grasses and berry bushes. In his 1634 book, *New England's Prospect,* William Wood, who lived in the Massachusetts Bay Colony, wrote:

> And wheras it is generally conceived that the woods grow so thicke, that there is no more cleare ground than is hewed out by the labour of man; it is nothing so; in many places divers acres being cleare, so that one may ride a hunting in most places of the land, if he will venture himselfe for being lost; there is no underwood saving in swamps and low grounds . . . for it being the custome of the Indians to burn the wood in November, when the grass is withered, and leaves dryed, it consumes all the underwood and rubbish, which otherwise

would over grow the country, making it unpassable, and spoil their much affected hunting; so that by this meanes in those places where the Indians inhabit, there is scarce a bush or bramble, or any cumbersome underwood to be seene in more champion ground.

Coastal savannah

Just as thousands of years of burning by Native Americans created an extensive prairie in parts of Wisconsin and Illinois—regions that now support forest—burning in New England in association with Native agriculture created a coastal savannah. A broken prairie ecosystem lined the coast from Portland, Maine, southward through Connecticut. In the region of Boston, the forest edge was reportedly six miles from the coast in some places. In *New Englands Plantation,* Francis Higginson wrote in 1630 about a hill near Boston that overlooked "thousands of acres" with "not a tree in the same." Building materials and fuel wood for early British settlement had to be attained on the forested islands of Boston Harbor.

The heath hen, an eastern relative of the prairie chicken and cousin of the grouse, thrived in this fire-managed savannah. It was so prolific in the coastal prairie that the first servants living in Boston had to negotiate that it would not be served more often than four times a week. Under British settlement and without Native American burning, the coastal prairie grew to forest, and the heath hen declined. It is ironic that fire, which had created the habitat of the heath hen, was also the cause of its eventual demise. In 1922, a fire destroyed the nesting area of the last heath hens, found in a remnant of coastal prairie on Nantucket. Following the fire and an unsuccessful breeding season, the population dropped below the critical level needed for group courtship in this species, and it soon went extinct.

It was a combination of clearing woodlands for Native agriculture and repeated fires that pushed forest margins from the New England coast. When abandoned garden plots were burned, they did not revert to forest but became open grassland or part of a savannah dotted by mature oaks or pines. Because the greatest concentrations of Native populations were along the coast, these were the areas that sustained the greatest combined impact from cultivation and fire. The same was true of New England's rivers. The rivers provided the main transportation routes to interior New England, along with a rich fishery and fertile alluvial soils. The rivers of southern and central New England, like the coasts, grew to be lined with grasslands known as *intervales*. This heritage has been preserved in the names of the towns that lie on the Connecticut River. Starting with Enfield, Connecticut, and traveling northward in Massachusetts, one passes through Springfield, Hatfield, Deerfield, Greenfield, and Northfield. The first colonists to settle these areas did so on "fields" generated by hundreds of years of Native agriculture and burning.

The common notion of New England's precolonial landscape as one of a forest primeval, where a squirrel could travel from treetop to treetop without ever touching the ground, is misguided. Within fifty years of the landing at Plymouth Rock, the Native American, fire-managed ecosystems of southern New England became a memory. With widespread disease decimating the Natives' numbers and Puritans forcing them from their ancestral lands, their historic use of fire as a management tool was lost and forgotten, as were the fire-generated savannahs and open, parklike forests. By 1700, the myth of a dense and impenetrable wilderness, tamed by the ax, became the heritage of the New England landscape.

Although early European explorers found the greatest evidence of fire in the densely populated areas of coastal southern New England, central New England had numerous fire-managed ecosystems, as well. Intervales were common on the Saco River in Maine, on the Merrimack River south of Plymouth, New Hampshire, and on the Connecticut River south of Wells River, Vermont. Open woodlands dominated by chestnut and oak were extensive in Worcester County in Massachusetts and observed by the first settlers in Northfield, Massachusetts; Winchester, New Hampshire; and Point Elizabeth, Maine. During the warmer and drier climate of six thousand years ago, when oak and pine were more numerous in central New England, Native burning in this region was probably even more extensive than it was just prior to European settlement.

Due to the presence of humans, fire has been, and continues to be, an important part of the tapestry that cloaks the landscape of central New England. Yet the magnificent precolonial woodlands, sculpted by fire, will never again be witnessed in this region. What must it have been like to walk through these massive-trunked stands of nut-producing trees? How different did one feel in those forests compared to the denser woodlands we find today? The people who could have shared their memories of that landscape are no more, but perhaps the history they left is an important lesson about the nature of our New England countryside—it is always changing. It has not been static since the departure of the Laurentide Ice Sheet some thirteen thousand years ago—and it is going to continue to change. These changes are in fact the primary authors that have inscribed their story onto the landscape of central New England—a fast-paced story of changing climates, logging, blights, blowdowns, and pasturing.

chapter two

OF JUNIPERS AND WEIRD APPLES

To many, woodland stone walls define the landscape of central New England. By one estimate, nearly one hundred thousand miles of stone walls crisscross its countryside. Yet the story of their origin is often lost to visitors and new residents. When walking Vermont's woodlands with friends from suburbia—landscapes with clear property boundaries in the form of fences and hedges—I ask them why they think the stone walls were built. They usually respond, "To mark woodland property boundaries." It is true that many of these walls delineate the extent of landownership, but if that were their sole purpose, they never would have been built.

Have you ever hurt your back while lugging stones, smashed a thumb while fitting them together, or rubbed your fingertips raw from lifting rock after rock? A strong stonemason can build ten to twenty feet of wall a day—if the stones are already at hand. If the stones must be fetched, the process takes even longer. To mark boundaries in a wooded landscape, it is far easier simply to blaze trees—marking them with paint or ax marks. So why would stone walls be constructed through woodlands? The answer is that they weren't. The stone walls that run through our forests, like the one depicted in this etching, were called stone fences. Their purpose was to keep farm animals in, or out, of the *open* landscapes they enclosed.

Can you identify a piece of evidence in this etching that confirms that this stone wall was constructed in a nonforested landscape? The squat, wide-spreading growth form of the two large trees that abut the wall tells us something important—that they did not grow up to reach the canopy of a forest, but rather grew out into open space. Trees growing in close proximity to other trees put their energy into racing toward the canopy to garner their share of limited sunlight. Trees growing in the open extend outward. This strategy accomplishes two things: It allows the tree to maximize the sunlight it can capture and to usurp space from future competitors. Only trees grown in the open have the wide-spreading form displayed in the etching. Some people refer to the large white pine on the right and the sugar maple on the left as *wolf trees,* for like a wolf, these open-grown trees often stand alone.

WOLF TREE AND YOUNG TREES

Besides its wide-spreading form, the white pine offers another clue that, as a young tree, it was growing in full sunlight. Pines, like all conifers, normally have single straight trunks that reach to their very tops. This tree has a trunk for only about six feet above ground level, which is then replaced by a number of main branches. Because the branches don't diverge at ground level, the pine can't be considered multiple trunked, but it does have an abnormal growth form. At a young age, something must have damaged its *terminal shoot* or *leader*—the single, upright branch at the very top of all coniferous trees. The trunks of pines and other conifers grow skyward through the development of this shoot. If the terminal shoot is injured, the lateral branches directly below it take on the role of new leaders, and the single trunk becomes replaced by multiple branches. Six feet being too high for the reach of a browsing animal, the best explanation is that this tree's terminal shoot was parasitized by the white pine weevil, a small insect that has a big impact on central New England's pines.

Weevils feed and lay their eggs in the terminal shoots of white pine. However, not any leader will do—the tree must be exposed to full sunlight and usually be less than forty feet tall. This ensures the weevils a warm and productive haven for larval development. Only the leaders of young pines growing in the open are heavily attacked by the white pine weevil, which in high numbers can kill the terminal shoot, allowing multiple-branched specimens to develop. As I write this, I can see out of my window a grove of forty-foot-tall white pines that covers three acres. Roughly one out of every two of these trees displays multiple branching ten to twenty feet off the ground. The pines in this weeviled stand are classic examples of trees that once grew in full sunlight, like the pine in the etching.

Judging from the six-inch diameters of the young trees in the foreground of this etching, this once open landscape has only recently become reforested. But when was it cleared? The four-foot diameters of the large wolf trees, which are well over one hundred years of age, allow us to place the original clearing of this landscape's forest sometime prior to 1900. During the nineteenth century, agricultural land was cleared for three different purposes: as either *cultivated land* for growing crops, *pastureland* for grazing animals, or *mowings* to produce hay.

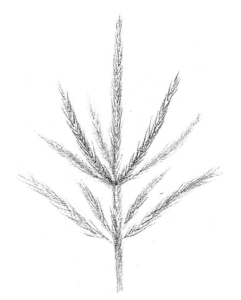

TERMINAL SHOOT

Examining the etching, can you tell which farming activity took place on this land? Maybe not, but there is evidence that will help us to determine whether it was cultivated, grazed, or mowed.

STONE WALL

The stone wall itself offers us a clue. If you have ever tended a vegetable garden in New England you might be able to guess what I am aiming at. Gardens that are free of vegetation during the winter produce something that continuously vegetated areas can't—an annual supply of stones that are brought to the surface by repeated freeze-and-thaw cycles. When vegetated ground, like a lawn, is frozen, it freezes as a total unit due to the network of interlacing roots that hold soil and rocks in place. But in areas free of vegetation and its associated roots, rocks move independently, being lifted by frost but falling not quite back to their original positions by thaw. Through this process, rocks migrate toward the surface. Luckily for lawn mowers, grass keeps these stones from surfacing, but in cultivated plots, you might think that rocks are capable of reproduction.

Because soil cannot be turned if it is full of stones—even ones smaller than the size of a fist—they are removed from cultivated plots, and what better place to take them to than the stone fence protecting the crops? Stone fences with numerous small rocks in their construction are a sure sign that adjacent land was used for cultivation. Fences composed solely of larger rocks, like the one in the etching, were built to keep livestock either in pastures or out of mowings, since neither of these agricultural activities necessitated the removal of small stones.

Juniper

So what was the land in this etching used for, mowing or pasture? The remnants of a coniferous shrub present in this landscape may help to answer this question. The upward arching branches arranged in radial formation are the skeletal remains of the common juniper, a woody plant intolerant of shade. From the looks of the branches on the specimens in the etching, which have lost their needles and fine twigs, these junipers have been dead for at least ten years. All of the smaller twigs have been shed, leaving the exposed main branches.

DEAD JUNIPER

In central New England, common juniper is found in only three sites: overgrazed pastures, the crevices of rock outcrops, and in poor, often sandy, substrates that support the growth of haircap moss (an eco-indicator of dry, nutrient-poor substrates, named for the hairy cap that covers its spore capsule). These sites share a common feature that allows juniper to grow: They support few other plants whose leaves would shade the young coniferous shrub. Mosses and lichens are the prominent plants on rock outcrops and in poor, dry sands, while in pastures, the grazing animals keep leafy plants cropped. During its first few years, juniper grows very slowly and needs sites free of competition from herbaceous plants. Once it reaches five to ten years of age and has developed a substantial root system, its growth rate accelerates, and no amount of herbaceous cover will suppress it.

Because the landscape in the etching is covered by snow, we can't be sure whether it supports haircap moss or displays creviced bedrock. Yet if there is exposed bedrock or a poor sandy substrate, wouldn't this also eliminate the possibility of a former hayfield, since neither would support a good stand of grasses? Not necessarily. The presence of extensive bedrock would eliminate the possibility of a former mowing, but nutrient-poor sands, if manured, could support productive hayfields. If neither exposed bedrock nor poor sands lie under the snowcover, then the juniper becomes a sure sign of an overgrazed pasture.

Weird apples

Because we can't assume this to be true, we must look to one more piece of evidence to decide finally whether this area was once mowing or pasture. To the right of the large sugar maple is an apple tree, and the lower portion of its contorted trunk supports a dense cluster of dead branches. I call apples with this growth form *weird apples* because of their gnarled appearance. The only explanation for their unusual form is heavy, repeated browsing during their youth; their presence confirms that the area in front of the stone wall was once a pasture.

Many shrubs that invade pastures have natural defenses to keep browsing animals at bay. The juniper is unpalatable, the hawthorn is armed with formidable thorns, as are roses, blackberries, and barberries. But the apple has no defensive strategy except tolerance—it is able to withstand sustained browsing by cows, goats, and sheep that would kill other species of trees. This heavy browsing deforms the young apple, and it becomes stunted with dense, twisting branches. But once the browsing stops, the apple begins to grow normally, becoming a tree. However, its pasture heritage is still visible in its contorted base that supports numerous dead, twisted branches.

WEIRD APPLE

One September morning, just after I first moved to Vermont, I wandered into an overgrazed pasture with ten-foot-wide mats of juniper. Scattered throughout one part of the pasture were bonsai-looking shrubs no more than two feet in height. Their branches were twisted and so densely packed that I could not see more than a couple of inches into their tangled masses. The leaves were all less than a half inch in length, and it took me five minutes to find a bud that I could examine with my hand lens. It was only then, when I saw the white wooly covering on the bud, that I realized I was looking at an apple tree. I guessed that the apple had been browsed for many years, and I was determined to age it.

The next day I returned with saw in hand and cut one of the bonsai apples. Once home, I sanded the cut and counted the rings. To my surprise, the twenty-two-inch-high shrub was thirty-two years old! My respect for the tenacity of this species was profoundly enhanced, and I now revere the apple as one of the toughest of trees.

Weird apples may be absent from an overgrazed pasture if larger apple trees are not close by, but common juniper will certainly be present. Berry-eating birds, particularly cedar waxwings, disperse juniper seeds far more effectively than mammals that ingest and disperse apple seeds. Many old pastures can be picked out on hillsides, even at a great distance, by their robust stands of common juniper. It is the most visible indicator of old, pastured landscapes in central New England. Along with wolf trees (which I prefer to call *pasture trees,* as they were often left to provide shade for the animals) and stone fences made of large rocks, these coniferous shrubs are a reminder of a past way of life that relied far more heavily on grazing animals than we do today.

The stone wall and remnant strands of barbed wire found in the etching give us more clues about the period during which this pasture was in use. The first pastures to be opened in central New England were bordered by zigzag, split-rail fencing. The construction of these fences took the least amount of energy investment; however, with the expansion of pastureland and associated decline of forests, stone fencing started replacing split-rail fencing in the early 1800s, with the majority of stone fences being constructed between 1810 and 1840. The invention and use of barbed wire in the 1870s replaced the laborious construction of stone fences. The stone wall and barbed wire tell us the pasture depicted in this etching was most likely cleared sometime in the early 1800s and remained active at least until the late 1800s.

In fact, we can actually place an even more recent date than the late 1800s on this pasture's abandonment. The young, six-inch-diameter trees in the foreground show no multiple trunking, which means that they have not been cut or burned and were most likely the first trees to invade the pasture. Because the juniper died about ten years ago, from the shade produced when these young trees formed a closed canopy, this pasture was probably "let go" twenty to thirty years ago. Therefore, during a period of over a hundred years, this landscape supported some form of grazing activity.

Succession

The process by which overgrazed pastures are reclaimed by forest is called *pasture succession*. In central New England, the initial stages are quite predictable and differ markedly from the succession of cultivated sites, mowings, or well-managed pastures (the latter are pastures whose stands of grasses are kept thick by light to moderate grazing and free of coarse weeds and woody plants by annual mowing).

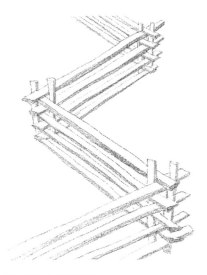

ZIGZAG FENCE

Pasture succession begins with overgrazing, which thins the turf and exposes the soil. These exposed areas become colonized by herbaceous plants that grow as prostrate, basal rosettes, which means that all of their leaves lie on the ground radiating from the top of the root system. This growth form is an effective strategy for avoiding the grasp of grazing animals. The majority of basal rosettes found in our pastures today, as well as in our lawns, are not native to central New England. They evolved in European grazing ecosystems that were established thousands of years prior to the colonization of the New World. When those ecosystems were transplanted in New England, so were the basal rosettes. The accidental introduction of these plants often came from seeds contained in the dirt that acted as ballast on colonial ships. The most common of these nonnative species are yarrow, sheep sorrel, strawberry, plantain, and hawkweed.

BASAL ROSETTE

Once basal rosettes establish, they are quickly followed by tall, unpalatable perennials like milkweed and goldenrod. Clumps of these coarse plants become nurseries for thorny shrubs such as hawthorn, rose, blackberry, and barberry. During their first few years, the thorns of these shrubs are pliable and of little defense; thus, they need to be hidden from grazers until they develop woody thorns. The unpalatable perennials serve to shelter the young shrubs from the mouths of the grazers.

In contrast to the thorny shrubs that take root in protected nurseries, common juniper grows in open areas with little herbaceous growth. Its resinous, unappetizing foliage replaces the need for thorns. These woody plants in turn act as *nurse shrubs* for invading trees. Most trees growing in the open are quickly browsed and, except for apples, will just as quickly perish. Those that happen to germinate in the middle of a clump of juniper, or in the midst of a multiflora rose, are protected and grow to tree size. Through this process they shade and eventually kill their nurse shrub—an unintentional but nonetheless unaltruistic act.

At this point in the process, as the pasture moves toward forest, succession becomes unpredictable—any mix of trees can reclaim an overgrazed pasture. One of the key factors affecting forest composition is the length of time that a pasture has been overgrazed. Those pastures that have witnessed decades of overgrazing and have established large mats of juniper and other shrubs will often succeed to a forest composed of a variety of trees. During the extended period of overgrazing, different species of trees seed into the nurse shrubs over successive years—white pine one year, red maple another, with sugar maple, black cherry, white ash, paper birch, and many more species colonizing the pasture in different years. All may be well represented in the young forest established on such a pasture.

Many of our local species of trees produce a huge crop of seeds every few years; these are called *mast years* ("mast" being another term for nuts). Trees have adapted this strategy to ensure the successful establishment of their offspring. Energy that could be put into seed production by the tree is instead placed into an "energy savings account" on an annual basis. For a number of years, the trees produce roughly the same amount of seed and thereby help to establish a set population level for animals that consume their seeds. When enough energy has been stored to produce a bumper crop, they celebrate with a mast year that produces as much as a hundredfold increase in seed production. The timing of the mast year is controlled by regional climate, so all members of a species within a large portion of central New England will mast at the same time. The birds or mammals that eat the seed have an overabundance of food, leaving ample seed to allow many young trees to establish.

Can you tell if the pasture in the etching was overgrazed for a long period of time? All of the young trees are of one species—sugar maple—and none of them is growing within the dead clumps of juniper. This tells us two things: This pasture didn't experience a prolonged period of overgrazing and it didn't have sufficient time to develop shrubs large enough to nurse a diverse mix of invading trees. The sugar maples probably germinated in the pasture shortly after its grazers were removed. The timing of abandonment most likely paralleled a mast year for sugar maple, allowing a pure stand to develop.

With the exception of plantations or species that are vigorous root sprouters like beech and aspen, pure stands of young trees owe their existence to a mast year. Some of the trees that have developed this strategy include oaks, maples, beeches, hickories, pines, birches, and ashes. This means that any one of a variety of pure stands can follow a pasture if the timing of abandonment falls during a mast year for a particular species of tree, and if the pasture has not been previously overgrazed for a long period of time. Thus, seed source is another important, but unpredictable, factor in the composition of a forest following pasturing. Therefore, former pastures can't necessarily be identified by the composition of the forest that replaces them.

The clues to pasture heritage are: stone fencing composed solely of large rocks, barbed wire, pasture trees, and residual pasture shrubs like juniper, hawthorn, and weird apples. Like the old stone fences that run through the forests of central New

England, the fraying warp and weft of a worn landscape tapestry, abandoned pastures leave apparitions of their forgotten pasts.

A LOOK BACK

To appreciate the changes wrought upon the countryside of central New England by the development of pasturelands, we need to trace the region's history through the last four centuries. The transition from the forested, Native American landscape of the early eighteenth century to one dominated by open pasture by the mid-nineteenth century was dramatic. Never in its history has central New England experienced such a rapid or profound change in its landscape.

At the time of Verrazano's first explorations of New England in the early 1500s, it is estimated that the region's Native population was roughly ninety to one hundred thousand. Within fifty years of the establishment of the Pilgrims' first colony at Plymouth, Massachusetts, in 1620, the Native population for all of New England had dropped to a few thousand. As in the rest of the Americas, the major cause of this dramatic decline in population was diseases of European origin, such as chicken pox and smallpox. Horrific epidemics swept through the entire Algonquin Nation—the more than two dozen tribes of New England and eastern Canada that shared the same linguistic heritage.

The first and worst of the recorded epidemics occurred during 1616 and 1617. It decimated Native populations all along the New England coast as far north as the Kennebec River in Maine and inland possibly as far as Vermont. Although the actual disease was never determined, it has been hypothesized that it was an outbreak of chicken pox, a disease rarely fatal to Europeans. To Native Americans, however, it was devastating. Whole villages were wiped out, and by the time the Pilgrims arrived just three years later, most coastal areas lay abandoned.

Europeans who witnessed this epidemic were shocked by the virulence of the disease in Native people, with only one out of every twenty infected Natives surviving. Because the disease had evolved thousands of years earlier in the Old World, people of European descent had developed an immunity to it, whereas most Native Americans had not. The same was true for the many other new diseases that wracked New England Natives during the seventeenth century. The next major epidemic was an outbreak of smallpox in 1633. It originated in the Connecticut River valley and spread to New York, Maine, and Quebec. In the next century, five more smallpox outbreaks continued to devastate New England's Native population. The epidemics not only brought high mortality rates, but they also substantially disrupted tribal structure. As many tribes were dramatically reduced in size, survivors migrated throughout New England, forming new, often ephemeral, tribal groups. Disease, it can be said, initiated the unraveling of the Algonquin Nation.

The dramatic reduction in Native populations, plus the associated disruption of tribal structure, set the stage for British colonization and ownership of New England. The argument used by the British for acquiring land during the seventeenth century was based on the European concept that unimproved land bore no stamp of ownership. Native Americans had a "natural right" to harvest the bounty of the land, but because the Natives did not enclose land, raise cattle, and have permanent settlements, they did not own it. Once their land was owned by colonists, even their natural right to the use of the land was lost. John Winthrop, in *Winthrop's Journal,* stated the British position quite clearly: "As for the natives in New England, they inclose noe Land, neither have any setled habytation, nor any tame Cattle to improve the land by, and soe have noe other but a Natural Right to those Countries." John Cotton did not even speak of natural rights for Native Americans. "We did not conceive that it is a just Title to so vast a Continent, to make no other improvement of millions of acres in it, but to burn it up for pastime." This quote, from *The Complete Writings of Roger Williams,* was a response to Williams's assertion that the Natives did own the land because they improved it through burning.

By 1670, most of southern New England had been colonized, and the migration of the British into central New England had begun. However, the remaining Algonquin population—numbering only a few thousand, but now with the support of the French—thwarted the colonial tide so effectively that no permanent settlements were established for almost another century.

In 1636 a trading post—for furs and as a base for further expansion up the Connecticut River valley—was created at the present site of Springfield, Massachusetts. By 1669 the British had established a settlement in Deerfield, Massachusetts, and by 1673 another in Northfield, Massachusetts. At the same time, British settlements were being established along the Merrimack River and the western coast of Maine.

But in 1675 the Western Abenaki—an affiliation of the Cowasuck, Missisquoi, Pennacook, Pigwacket, and Sokoki tribes of present-day New Hampshire and Vermont—began to actively resist British colonial expansion. Western Abenaki warriors, in association with displaced warriors from southern New England tribes, drove the British out of the Merrimack River valley north of Nashua and the Connecticut River valley north of Deerfield. This endeavor to take back their ancestral lands initiated eighty-five years of sporadic fighting, with the French supporting the Western Abenaki in a joint effort against the British.

By 1713 most of the remaining Western Abenaki were concentrated in two settlements—at Missisquoi on Lake Champlain and St. Francis in Quebec—their combined population probably less than a thousand. This small remnant, made up of individuals from many tribes and with continued French backing, blocked British expansion for another fifty years. Their most famous warrior, Grey Lock, led raiding parties as far south as Northampton, Massachusetts, and was greatly feared by the settlers of the Connecticut River valley. Repeated advancements and abandonments of British settlements occurred until 1744, finally culminating in seven years of warfare known as the French and Indian War. This war began in 1753 and was named for the last alliance of the French and the remaining Algonquin tribes in their fight against the British. With the defeat of the French at Montreal in 1760 and in the face of an ever-expanding British militia, the Natives fought no more. With eighty-five years of conflict at an end, the colonial floodgates were opened, and "the great swarming time," as historian Charles E. Clark calls it, had begun.

The great swarming time

The mass migration of the British began up the Connecticut and Merrimack River valleys of Vermont and New Hampshire, as well as along the coast of Maine. In 1761, seventy-eight new towns were granted in the Connecticut River valley alone. From their initial river settlements, the British spread into the rest of central New England, so that by 1790 all of the region's present towns had been established. After the fall of Montreal and within fifteen years of the 1763 Treaty of Paris, when France formally surrendered what is now the northeastern United States to England, 150,000 new colonists had settled in Vermont, New Hampshire, and Maine. By 1791, there were 85,000 people in Vermont alone, swelling to 217,000 by 1810.

This rapid colonization brought dramatic changes to the landscape of central New England. The first settlements were often established in fields, first cleared by Natives, or on abandoned beaver meadows, which required little clearing and offered good forage for livestock. If these were not available, upland areas where forests were less dense, and local environments less chilly than valley bottoms, were cleared and then settled.

Men would usually prepare a homestead over a period of two to four summers and then be joined by their families. During preparation, the men cleared land by ax—up to three acres a summer—built log cabins, and prepared fencing for animals. The first fences were often built with large logs or intertwining stumps, which had been uprooted to create mowings and sites for cultivation. The most effective way to clear land for fields was to chop down trees late in the summer, at the close of the growing season to restrict stump-sprouting in hardwoods, and burn the site the next spring before things "greened up." Clearing the land of forest not only prepared it for agriculture, but also produced a crop of potash, or wood ash, from burning the cleared trees. Approximately two tons of potash were produced for every acre cleared of forest, enough to make one hundred pounds of soap or gunpowder.

These first homesteads were self-sufficient and produced few market products. Free time was an almost unknown concept to the early settlers. If all the day's chores were completed, there was always more land to be cleared, more stumps to be pulled, and more rocks to be removed from fields. These early settlers worked hard from sunrise to sunset. Without the Sabbath, which forbade work one day a week, they might have worked themselves to death. Little could the inhabitants of central New England have known that Napoleon's victory over Portugal in 1809 was about to change drastically the nature of these self-sufficient farms—and, as a result, the landscape of the entire region.

Sheep fever

Before losing to Napoleon, the Portuguese aristocracy had bred a special kind of sheep called the merino. It was highly regarded for its ample fleece, which produced a very soft, high-quality wool. As there was great worldwide demand for the wool, the Portuguese rigorously protected their interests by placing an embargo on the export of this breed from Portugal. With their defeat, however, came loss of control of the merino, which opened the door in 1810 for William Jarvis, then American Consul to Portugal, to import four thousand of the sheep to his Weathersfield, Vermont, farm.

Following the War of 1812, the U.S. government imposed a tariff law on English goods, including woolens, and a thirty-year period of "sheep fever" took hold of central New England. In his book *Social Ferment in Vermont 1791–1850,* David Ludlum writes, "A wool craze swept the region, a mania as powerful as any religious fanaticism." Between 1810 and 1820, the number of textile mills in the region processing merino wool multiplied threefold. With the increased demand for wool came a dramatic rise in the merino population. By 1824, Vermont's 4,000 sheep had increased to 475,000. By 1836, its sheep population hit 1.1 million, reaching a peak of 1.7 million in 1840. The same trend took place in New Hampshire, with a peak of more than 600,000 sheep by 1840.

To support all of these sheep, the landscape changed dramatically. The majority of the countryside was cleared of forest to create pasturage, and few sites were excluded from this process—steep hillsides, ridgetops, and even heavily bouldered areas were used. By 1840, approximately 75 percent of the region's landscape had been converted to open land for agricultural use, the bulk of it sheep pasture. Extensive stone fencing designed to keep the sheep in their pastures also began to crisscross the landscape. Prior to 1810, the majority of fences were made of wood. Stump fences were eventually replaced by split-rail, zigzag fencing, but with the loss of forest, wood for fencing became scarce, and piles of rock that had been removed from agricultural land became a new resource for fence construction.

When the stones were close at hand, the industrious settlers could lay ten to twenty feet of stone wall a day. To contain sheep, the walls had to be four and a half feet high. Often wooden rails or even brush was laid on the stones to add to the wall's height. Maintaining high fencing was enforced by law, as free-roaming sheep could ruin people's crops. Fence wardens patrolled townships, and fines for inadequate fencing were common.

Because the bulk of these stone fences were built in a thirty-year period between 1810 and 1840, and the mass of stone in these walls was greater than that of the Great Pyramids of Egypt, it seems fair that central New England's stone fences be considered the eighth wonder of the world. The great irony of this Herculean effort to clear the land and surround it with stone walls was that this pastoral landscape was exceedingly short-lived. By 1840 the sheep farms were being abandoned in wholesale fashion. By 1900 more than half of the cleared land was growing back to forest, shrouding thousands of miles of stone walls, like the one seen in the etching at the beginning of this chapter.

A number of factors contributed to this rapid recovery from "sheep fever." The soils that underlay the pastures were thin due to previous glacial activity, and therefore susceptible to erosion. In their zeal to produce as much wool as possible, farmers overstocked their pastures, and by the 1830s erosion caused by sheep was substantial. Not only did productivity of the sheep farms rapidly decline, but also the region's streams and rivers became overburdened by silt. Some of the worst floods in central New England's history took place in this era as waterways, choked by the residue of overgrazing, flowed over their banks.

The impact of nineteenth-century "sheep fever" is still around us. In many places, sheep pastured on ridgetops caused such massive erosion that they exposed extensive bedrock, much of it still visible more than a century later. Although erosion following blowdowns and fire can also create bare outcroppings of rock, a large percentage of the exposed bedrock found in the region today owes its presence to past overgrazing by sheep.

Just as a mass migration into central New England followed the end of the French and Indian Wars, so did a mass exodus to the West begin as New England farming families looked for greener pastures. The decline of farm productivity in New England fueled the development of transportation routes to the rich and unglaciated soils of the Ohio River valley. The Erie Canal was opened in 1825, and rail service to the West followed shortly thereafter. By 1850, 100,000 Vermonters—almost one-half the state's population—had moved west. Orford, New Hampshire, which had a peak population of 1,829 people in 1830, dropped to 1,406 by 1850 and to 916 by 1890. This trend was widespread throughout the region. (In fact, most rural towns in central New England presently have fewer residents than they did in 1840!)

The first farms to be abandoned were the "hill farms," founded on the thin and poorer soils of the region's ridges. The "valley farms" developed on the deeper alluvial soils of the river bottomland continued to function as market farms, but many shifted from sheep to dairy cattle after the 1850s. Central New England farmers could not compete with their western counterparts in wool production, but they could supply milk products to the mill towns that had sprung up during the sheep craze of the early nineteenth century and continued to produce textiles.

The dairy farms that most people identify as typically New England—farms with herds of fifty to one hundred cows—did not appear until after the Civil War. By that time associated dairy systems developed to process and market milk products, with the first in Vermont being established in 1854. Over 90 percent of the pastures we see in the region today are a continuation of this dairying heritage, but these dairy farms are disappearing almost as rapidly as their sheep-grazing predecessors did in the mid-nineteenth century. Today's declining milk prices are pushing dairy operations to grow ever bigger to be competitive. This trend is easily accommodated in the Plains states and California, where farms usually cover thousands of acres. But in New England, where dairy farms are only a few hundred acres in size and herds are smaller, farmers often can't produce enough milk to remain viable.

Farm abandonment and the associated loss of pastures over the past 150 years has created the single most obvious historical pattern in the region's landscape. The succession of pasture to forest is primarily responsible for the composition of today's woodlands. Wherever we venture in the forests of central New England, the stamp of abandoned pasture is close at hand. Stone fences, barbed wire, and pasture trees tell of a dramatic period in the history of the central New England landscape.

chapter three

A STUDY IN STUMPS

The stumps in this etching, flecked by spring sunlight and in contrast to the even-aged, pure stand of hemlock, are striking. Weathered and worn, they give distinction to the forest understory. Yet I doubt the loggers responsible for cutting these trees had any thoughts of future forest floor aesthetics. When festooned with lichens, moss, and fungi, stumps are lilliputian ecosystems inhabited by countless organisms, making them worthy of close inspection and admiration. But stumps can also be appreciated in another way: For people who learn how to read them, they accurately record forest history.

Perhaps it's already evident that this chapter is going to focus on logging, the most common form of forest disturbance in our region. A person would be hard pressed to enter a central New England forest and not find evidence of cut trees. Unlike the two previous etchings, this one depicts an actual forest—one that exists in the town of Vernon, Vermont. It was chosen because its stumps tell an especially clear story of its logging history.

You may be able to recognize that this forest has been logged by its flat-topped stumps. However, the stumps tell us far more than just that. How many times has the area been logged? Which species of trees were cut? When and specifically why were the trees cut? The stumps hold the answers to all these questions. Before reading further, see if you can identify how many different kinds of stumps can be seen in the etching.

We can see that some of the stumps retain bark and appear to be more rotted just beneath their bark than in their centers (represented in the etching by the lighter coloration of these stumps' centers). A second group of stumps are barkless, gray in coloration, and appear to be the opposite—more rotted in their centers than on the outside. These latter stumps are also coppiced (they have multiple trunks), which suggests they are hardwood trees that were exposed to either fire or logging prior to their last cutting. In order to tell how many times this forest has been logged, we need to know if past cutting created the coppiced trees. Is there any evidence that can confirm whether it was fire or logging that caused the multiple trunking?

If we knew the size of the original trees, we could make an educated guess as to which was more likely. Large trees, with their thicker bark, are usually resistant to being killed by fire but are highly valued for timber. If all the multiple-trunked stumps in the etching were generated by the removal of large trees, it would be strong support for logging. Luckily, there is a way to estimate the original size of trees that have stump-sprouted and become multiple trunked. Because the sprouts all grew on the outside of the former stump, we can approximate the diameter of the original tree by connecting the centers of each stump-sprout and creating an imaginary circle near

BARKLESS, COPPICED STUMP

ground level. When we do this with the multiple-trunked stumps in the Vernon forest, we see that the original trees must have been three to four feet in diameter. Even a hot fire could not kill all the trees of this size, making logging a far more reasonable guess as the cause of these multiple-trunked trees.

Knowing that logging created multiple-trunked trees that were subsequently cut again, we now have evidence of two cuttings. Is there other evidence suggesting more than two cuttings? To answer this question we need to determine whether the two species of trees, represented by the stumps retaining bark and those that are multiple trunked, were logged at the same time. If we could identify the species of trees that were cut, we could answer this question based on the rates at which their stumps decay.

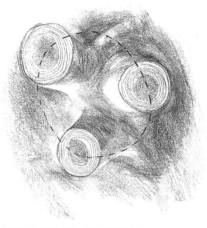

ESTIMATING ORIGINAL STUMP SIZE

Stump decay

Examine the bark on those stumps that have it. It is sound and free of moss and lichen growth. The pattern of this bark looks similar to the bark of the overstory hemlocks. Could these stumps be hemlock? It is a strong guess, and there is evidence to support it. Hemlock bark is very rot resistant and supports little growth of moss or lichens, just like the bark on the etching's stumps. This is due to a large amount of tannin in the bark—acidic compounds produced by plants to protect their tissues from being eaten. Tannins were also used in the tanning of hides to make leather. Because of its high tannin content, hemlock bark was the mainstay of the tanning industry until the early twentieth century and has the most rot-resistant bark of any tree in central New England.

STUMP WITH BARK

Another feature that helps us identify these stumps as hemlock is their solid center. All coniferous trees—hemlock, pine, and spruce—that lack rot prior to being cut decay from the outside in. Like broad-leaved trees, conifers have two kinds of wood composing their trunks. The outer zone is known as sapwood (which in conifers carries viscous, resinous sap); the inner, heartwood. The heartwood of coniferous trees has three qualities that allow it to have a greater resistance to wood-boring insects and fungal decay than sapwood. Heartwood has less carbohydrate storage and lower porosity, meaning it holds less water than sapwood. These qualities make heartwood less palatable to wood borers and reduce fungal growth rates. But more importantly, the heartwood of conifers stores substances toxic to insects and fungi, keeping them at bay until these substances are degraded or leached from the log.

Even more rot resistant than the heartwood of a conifer's trunk are coniferous knots—the very dense bases of limbs encased by sapwood. I discovered this shortly after moving to Vermont, when I observed some white pine logs that had been cut, skidded into a nearby pasture, and for some reason never hauled to the mill. These logs had long since lost their bark and had been lying on the ground for probably forty years. What puzzled me about the logs was that they all had branches about six inches long. Why would someone cut timber and skid it to a loading site without first cutting the branches flush to the sawlogs? And if the branches weren't removed, why didn't they snap off during skidding? It eventually occurred to me that these were not branches left at the time of cutting, but rather the bases of branches that had been encased in sapwood. Forty years of sapwood decay had left these knots exposed and still hard as nails.

HEARTWOOD AND SAPWOOD

Rot-resistant hardwood trees exhibit a pattern opposite to that of coniferous species in that their outer sapwood is far more resistant to decay than their heartwood, so they rot from the inside out. However, most species of hardwoods are rot-prone, like the birches, maples, and beeches. Stumps and logs of these species all rot uniformly throughout and quite quickly, decaying completely within twenty-five to thirty years. Maples and beeches commonly develop the black fungus discussed in the first chapter, which makes them appear as if they have been charred.

The multiple-trunked stumps in the etching are rotting from the inside out; thus, they must be either oak, locust, or American chestnut—central New England's rot-resistant hardwoods. It is the long, vertical check lines—cracks that result when wood shrinks—and weathered, light brown wood that distinguish these stumps (as well as the downed, curved limb at the left) as American chestnut, the most rot-resistant tree in central New England. Identifying the multiple-trunked stumps as American chestnut and the others as hemlock will now help us tell how many times this forest has been logged, as well as giving us clues to when these cuttings took place.

Because American chestnut decays from the inside out, the present diameter of the cut stumps is similar to that of the living trunks at the time of cutting—or about one foot. Why would someone cut all the multiple trunks of the chestnut when they were relatively small? The most likely answer is that these trees were salvaged when an accidentally introduced fungal blight killed just about all of the American chestnut in New England prior to 1920. (The dramatic story of this blight will be told more completely in another chapter.) The cutting also ages these stumps at seventy to eighty years, far longer than any hemlock stump could hope to exist.

I first learned to age decayed hemlock stumps while walking a neighbor's land a few years ago. On a hillock just south of an old barbed-wire fence that separates our woodlands stands one of the most dramatic hemlocks I have ever encountered. Its gnarled, five-foot-wide trunk and low-spreading multiple branches told me this hemlock was a pasture tree that grew alone at the top of this hill centuries ago. While approaching the tree, I observed a number of hemlock stumps, many of which were reduced to rings of hemlock bark with hollow, completely decayed centers. The flat cut of a saw was still clearly visible on the bark's top. Two of these stumps caught my attention because I noticed they were still alive and growing!

On one side of each stump, a crescent of new wood had grown just inside of the bark to a height about two inches above the old cut mark. Just as a tree will try to heal a basal scar, these stumps were attempting to heal wounds that had amputated everything growing above them. With no leaves to capture sunlight, how were the stumps growing? The only explanation is that the roots of the stump had grafted onto the roots of surrounding hemlocks before the tree was cut. Root grafting in trees is not uncommon, especially in thin substrates where roots regularly grow into one another. The surviving hemlocks supplied the stump with enough carbohydrates to continue growth at a minimal level.

I immediately wanted to know how long these cut stumps had been growing. Luckily, hemlock wounds can be aged by visible annual growth lines that form in the new bark—covering injuries. No tree in New England can better record the date of past damage than a hemlock. The annual lines on the new bark of these stumps recorded their cutting at thirty-eight years in the past. It had taken almost forty years for the wood of the stump to completely decay. Without wood to support them, the hollow rings of old bark will probably last only a decade more, placing the maximum longevity for hemlock stumps less than two feet in diameter at fifty years; larger stumps can last far longer. How long the root-grafted stumps can keep growing I do not know. But I have encountered hemlock knobs rising from the ground and imagined they were some form of root growth. I am now inclined to think they are the root-grafted, living remains of cut hemlocks whose original stumps and bark have completely rotted away.

With the information that has been presented thus far, is it possible to answer the questions raised at the start of this chapter: What trees were cut, when were they cut, and why were they cut? If the one-foot-diameter, multiple-trunked chestnuts were cut prior to 1920, their large forefathers must have been cut about thirty to forty years earlier—the time it takes to grow a one-foot-wide stump-sprout. This suggests that a magnificent forest dominated by American chestnut occupied this site following the Civil War and was logged around 1880. More than one hundred years later the decaying, moss-covered mounds (encircled by the multiple-trunked stumps, plus one without stump-sprouts in the middle of the etching) of the original chestnuts' stumps remain visible.

Following the second cutting of the chestnut around 1920, hemlock, which was probably already established in the understory, grew to dominate this forest. A third cutting to thin the hemlock was carried out within the last forty years. This can be surmised from the hemlock stumps that still display heartwood, something they rarely do after forty years of decay.

MOSS-COVERED MOUND

The Vernon, Vermont, forest depicted in the etching sports only two kinds of stumps. One has the most rot-resistant bark, the other the most rot-resistant wood, of all species found in New England. It is their ability to resist decay that allows these stumps to record accurately a logging history more than a century old. Although logging is ever present in our region's forests, few woodlands record its history as clearly as the forest in this etching. Yet with practice, rot-resistant hardwoods, rot-prone hardwoods, and coniferous stumps can be identified and approximately aged. Such a study in stumps illuminates how logging has changed the nature of New England's forests.

A LOOK BACK

One hundred years is a long time to be able to interpret a woodland's logging history. Yet the cutting of central New England's forests goes back more than 350 years. During that time, decay has eliminated all direct evidence for most of the region's historical logging; therefore, important questions remain. How did the unlogged forests of central New England differ from those of today? Which species of trees were most harvested by the early colonists? To what degree has logging altered the composition and structure of our regional forests? Fortunately, written accounts record the early cutting of central New England's forests and provide answers to our questions.

When the first Europeans began to settle New England in the early 1600s, some Native people thought they had traveled across the ocean in search of wood. Extirpation of wood within a reasonable walking distance of a village was the major factor that motivated Native tribes to relocate their settlements, so to them it seemed reasonable that this would be the case for the Europeans. In fact, this was not far from the truth. But while Natives were interested in wood primarily as a source of fuel, Europeans were interested in its potential for timber. The impact of colonial logging on the landscape of central New England was of a different nature from that of Native cutting.

The first British to explore the interior forests of central New England were enthralled by expansive tracts of old-growth forest. Chestnut, oak, beech, and maple were abundant, but the tree that most captivated their attention was the majestic white pine. They simply had never seen a tree of such stature. And although white pine continues to be a hallmark of the central New England forest, with more modest populations being found in southern and northern New England, its grandeur as a forest tree is not what it once was.

It is hard to imagine what four-hundred-year-old groves of this tree must have looked like, for today few white pines reach half this age. At two hundred years they tower above all other species by more than fifty feet and attain diameters of up to five feet. Yet these 150-foot giants have just reached their adulthood. Given another two centuries of growth, they would tower well over two hundred feet and reach diameters of up to eight feet. Some white pines encountered by the early colonists were recorded at heights of up to 220 feet, trees whose stature would fit nicely in a Pacific Northwest old-growth forest but seem out of place in our current image of a New England woodland.

Unlike the pine forests we find in New England today, which are common on uplands that were once pasture, many of the precolonial white-pine groves were found in lowland, riparian sites along central New England's major watercourses. The Kennebec, Saco, Merrimack, and Connecticut Rivers were the realm of the white pine. In these moist, silty, or sandy substrates, pines grew vigorously. Growing with elevated river terraces at their backs or in ravines cut by tributaries, the pines found wind-protected havens. Because these mammoth trees grew more than one hundred feet above their companions, protection from windthrow and lightning strikes was a necessity.

To stand at the base of a 150-foot white pine, such as those just off Route 103 in Bradford, New Hampshire, or just off the Livermore Road to the north of Waterville Valley, New Hampshire, is an awe-inspiring experience. How much more inspiring would it be to stand in the open understory of a four-hundred-year-old grove of this eastern giant? None of us will know, because these redwoodlike central New England forests were the first to be clear-cut in the fledgling colonial logging industry.

The cutting of white pines, primarily as masts for ships of the British navy, began in 1654 in the Piscataqua River watershed, which currently separates coastal New Hampshire from Maine. Ships designed specifically to haul pine masts carried up to thirty trees at a time back to England. By 1691 the cutting of pine for the British navy and for colonial use had reduced the numbers of easily accessible large pine enough to prompt the British Admiralty to pass a new law for the Massachusetts Bay Colony Charter. It mandated that all white pine twenty-four inches and larger in diameter (measured one foot above ground level) be reserved for the navy.

Under the king's command, all such trees were blazed with the mark of a broad arrow. Three blows with an ax produced a symbol that probably looked more like a large turkey track than an actual arrow. Although the fine for cutting one of these trees was one hundred pounds, the lack of enforcement did little to curb unauthorized cutting and use of these superb pines. By the early 1700s, all white pines were placed under the king's protection, yet indiscriminate cutting of the region's most majestic trees continued, reaching ever deeper into the river drainages of central New England. This gave rise to the following statement by Timothy Dwight in his 1821 book, *Travels in New England and New York:* "There is reason to fear that this noblest of all vegetable productions will be unknown in its proper size and splendor to future inhabitants of New England." This was prophetic, for not one of these huge white pines remains.

As Native tribes were forced to surrender central and northern New England, the cutting of riparian white pine moved steadily northward until the middle of the nineteenth century, when almost all trees of grand stature were gone. At this point the logging of large white pines moved westward to the lake states of Michigan and Wisconsin, to be repeated there. Yet this did not mark the end of the logging history of central New England's white pine.

The migration of clear-cutting to the lake states happened to coincide with the westward movement of the sheep industry and large-scale pasture abandonment in central New England. The deserted pastures created an extensive new ecosystem with plenty of sunlight and exposed soil, one especially accommodating to the establishment of white pine. Thus, after two centuries of land use the realm of the white pine in central New England shifted dramatically from lowland, riparian sites to upland abandoned pastures.

Sustained yield

By the beginning of the twentieth century, many former pastures supported almost pure stands of sixty-year-old white pine. Although not comparable in size to their riparian ancestors, these fast-growing trees had reached marketable dimensions. A second logging boom began. In addition to leading a resurgence in the central New England logging industry, the regeneration of white pine also coincided with the development of a new approach to forestry: *sustained yield*—the use of forestry management techniques to produce timber on a continued basis.

Prior to the twentieth century, all logging in North America was based on the clear-cutting of virgin forests; once the trees were eliminated, the cutting simply migrated west. The idea that forests could be managed to yield timber on a consistent basis was new to the region, and white pine became a demonstration species. Selective cutting to generate uneven-aged stands and other practices were introduced to maintain pine production. Between 1900 and 1930, white pine rose once again to become the mainstay of the central New England logging industry.

However, during the 1930s disease and wind damage (to be examined in future chapters) dramatically affected the region's pinelands, and management of this species lost a substantial following. A wonderful set of dioramas at the Harvard Forest Museum in Petersham, Massachusetts, outlines the history of the white pine presented in the previous three paragraphs. The dioramas are skillful renderings of the landscape history of central New England. White pine remains a key component of the region's logging industry, but is unlikely ever to reclaim its former dominant role.

Forestry practices have continued to change through this century. Although foresters still operate under the concept of sustained yield of timber, new values relating to sustaining wildlife, water quality, and, most recently, biodiversity have been included in forest management practices. However, the concept of sustained yield remains theoretical. We do not have enough management experience to say that our present practices can produce sustained yields for another few centuries.

From an evolutionary perspective, logging is a new form of disturbance to our woodlands. It differs from fire, blowdown, and beaver activity in that a certain amount of nutrients and biomass is removed from the system in the wood that is harvested. Of critical concern is the removal of two essential plant nutrients in the wood products: calcium and magnesium. We know that to sustain a fertile garden, nutrients removed by harvesting vegetables have to be returned in the form of compost, manure, or fertilizer; otherwise, vegetable production drops off.

In all forests, some calcium and magnesium are continuously lost as water leaches these nutrients into streams. The weathering of rocks in the soil and deposition of calcium and magnesium from the atmosphere replace the lost nutrients. The question is whether logging removes these essential nutrients at rates faster than they can be replaced by weathering and deposition. At this point the answer to this question is unclear, and because three or four cuttings are the most that any parcel in the region has yet experienced, it is too early to tell if our forestry practices are *truly* sustainable. Although the sustainability of logging remains an open question, logging practices over the past few hundred years have changed the nature of our central New England forests. Two of these changes are readily observable: Our forests have witnessed a shift in species composition, and their structure has become more homogeneous.

Certain species of trees are less common today than they were in the past, most notably oak, hickory, and cherry. All, being highly valued hardwoods, have been harvested at rates greater than their ability to regenerate. Others, such as red maple and hemlock, have dramatically increased due to low market demand. Along with shifts in species composition, our forests display a simpler structure. Most stands are even-aged. Old trees are rare. The amount of downed woody debris—an important component of the ecosystem for many species—is often less than it was in old-growth, precolonial forests free of fire. Large downed trees are a haven for fungi, beetles, grubs, ants, salamanders, plus a host of other organisms and are critical for healthy forest ecosystem interactions.

The logging of woodlands will continue to be the region's most common form of forest disturbance. For social and economic reasons it would be foolish to curtail this practice, and if the shift in management objectives continues to expand from one based solely on the production of wood products, as it was at the start of the century, to one based on ecosystem health, sustainability may become a reality.

Recently, the tallest tree in the lower forty-eight states east of the Continental Divide was found in the Great Smoky Mountains. At 207 feet, it is comforting to know that at least one majestic white pine still remains. With some far-reaching vision, maybe we can preserve some of central New England's wind-protected, riparian groves so that in a few hundred years our descendants will be able to walk beneath the true monarchs of the New England forest.

chapter four
NECTRIA

The most striking feature of this chapter's etching is the contrasting bark textures found in its trees. They highlight the tight, smooth, gray bark of the large American beech centered in this forest. No other tree in New England has bark quite like that of the beech. Of all the northerly deciduous trees—maples, cherries, ashes, oaks, and birches—with which it associates, beech is the only species to have completely smooth bark as a full-sized tree. The barks of maples and cherries are scaled, those of ashes and oaks ridged, and the bark of birches peels or forms plates (on black birch). Why is the bark texture of American beech so different?

As we learned from the discussion of fire-tolerant trees in chapter 1, bark texture is not just a random result of tissue development, but an adaptation to environmental conditions. Thick, scaly barks protect underlying cambial tissues from heat damage. But fire is not the only temperature-related phenomenon for which northern deciduous trees need protective bark. They also need protection from the heating effect of winter sunlight. And they receive this protection in the form of either rough bark textures or light colorations.

FROST CRACK

Intuitively, it seems that trees should benefit from exposure to winter sunlight and not need to protect themselves from it. To see why sunlight can be a problem for deciduous trees in winter, think of a still, cold January afternoon in central New England. The sun is low on the horizon, the temperature is five below zero, and a deciduous tree stands at the edge of a snow-covered meadow. As sunlight falls directly on the tree's trunk, it heats the bark and the underlying wood. If the bark is dark, its temperature may rise to over seventy degrees. When solid materials like bark and wood heat up, they expand. The sun then dips below the horizon and the bark quickly begins to cool and contract, but the insulated wood beneath the bark retains its warmth longer and contracts at a much slower pace. As a result of the bark's faster rate of contraction, it cracks open, forming a wound called a *frost crack*. Each time frost cracking is repeated, the wound opens a little wider and works its way deeper into the wood. After a number of years a frost crack can extend to the very heart of a tree's trunk, weakening it enough that wind or snow load can snap it.

Coniferous trees—like spruce—that hold their leaves throughout the year don't have this problem because their branches shade the trunk. Unable to produce protective shade during the winter, deciduous trees have developed adaptations in their barks to guard against frost cracking.

One of these adaptations is rough bark texture in the form of scales, ridges, or plates. These bark projections act like the metal fins on a radiator, releasing heat to the surrounding air rather than the underlying wood. Another adaptation is light bark coloration to reflect sunlight. It is not an accident that the two species of deciduous trees having the most northerly ranges in North America—paper birch and trembling aspen—also have the lightest bark colorations. In these high latitudes, the potential for frost cracking is great. The path the winter sun follows is just above the horizon, so tree trunks exposed to sunlight receive a direct dose. As daytime temperatures can be a bitter twenty to thirty degrees below zero, bark contraction following sunset would be rapid in trees having dark bark. The light bark of paper birch and trembling aspen is an adaptation to high-latitude winter sunlight.

The light gray bark of American beech is a needed adaptation for reflecting winter sunlight since it lacks rough bark to radiate heat into the surrounding air. But this does not answer our original question: Why has beech developed smooth bark when all of its northern deciduous associates have rough bark?

American beech is a member of the Fagaceae—a family of trees that evolved in the tropics. A problem tropical trees must contend with is *epiphytes*—plants that grow on trees—like mosses, ferns, and bromeliads. Individually, epiphytes do not harm their host trees, but in large aggregations their weight can break branches and even topple whole trees. An adaptation to thwart an epiphyte's ability to find a "roothold" is smooth bark. Although beech grows far into Quebec, it retains its tropical adaptation of smooth bark, compensating it with light coloration to reflect winter sunlight.

The beech's bark, particularly in large specimens like the one centered in the etching, dramatically stands out among its forest companions. Each year I take my Antioch plant communities class to a small section of old-growth forest in southeastern Vermont. A number of trees in this forest are well over three feet in diameter, including a four-foot-diameter hemlock and a seven-foot-diameter sugar maple (a pasture tree on the edge of the old-growth forest). But it is the three-foot-diameter beech, with its austere yet elegant bark, that most captivates the students' attention. Sadly, as this chapter will point out, majestic specimens like the beech centered in the etching are becoming rare.

A close examination of the etching reveals numerous trees whose barks are cracked and pitted—all of them American beech. Some display long, vertical scars; others have snapped in half, their tops decaying on the ground. What has happened to reduce the vigor of so many beech in this forest?

CRACKED BEECH BARK

The presence of long, vertical scars may suggest disturbance by logging or fire. As explained in chapter 1, the removal of bark by skidding logs through a forest or the burning of fuel pockets adjacent to trees can create basal scars. If decay-producing organisms invade these wounds, the scars sometimes expand up the trunk, like the scars in the etching, to heights well above the original basal scar. Thinking back to the chapters on logging and fire, what evidence other than basal scars should we look for to confirm if either disturbance occurred in this forest? If logging was recent, cut stumps should be noticeable. If hardwoods were cut, multiple-trunked trees should be present. Beech heat-killed by fire would die and decay on the stump, like some of the trees in the etching. Yet fire, like logging, should also generate the sprouting of coppiced growth at the base of the dying trees. But the complete lack of cut stumps and any coppiced growth is strong evidence that neither logging nor fire has occurred in this woodland.

When numerous trees in a forest are dying or standing dead, and evidence of logging or fire is not at hand, you are seeing the work of *forest pathogens*—insects and diseases that kill trees. The cause of the beech's appearance in this etching is just one episode in a relatively recent, alarming series of accidentally introduced forest blights.

The malady affecting these beech is called *beech bark scale disease* and is caused by a tiny scale insect in association with the fungus *Nectria coccinea*. The relationship between these two species is *commensalistic*—an interaction where one organism is benefited and the other is not affected by the association. In this commensalism, the scale insect inadvertently carries the fungus's spores and inoculates them into beech trees, a benefit to the *Nectria coccinea* but of no consequence to the scale insect.

Because adult scale insects can't fly far, they rely on wind to carry them into new forests. The first sign that a beech has been infected can be found in the fall. This is the time of year when adults, attached to the bark, cover themselves in a white, waxy coating that makes them look like minute tufts of cotton. The tufts are not much larger than a period on this page, with the scale insect inside being too small to be seen with the unaided eye.

The adults overwinter on the bark, protected by their woolly blanket to temperatures as low as thirty degrees below zero. (Stands of beech found above two thousand feet often lack evidence of beech scale blight due to colder winter temperatures found there.) In early summer, eggs are laid on the bark; larvae develop, reaching adulthood in the fall. Some of the adults remain on the original tree, increasing the scale insects' population density; others migrate in search of new trees. If the beech they emigrate from was infected by the *Nectria* fungus, the scale insects will accidentally carry the fungal spores to their new host trees.

Throughout their lives, scale insects feed on the tree's sap. They pierce the bark with their *stylets*—minute, needlelike mouthparts used to suck the sap. In areas where they are concentrated, their feeding creates microscopic wounds, allowing the introduction of the *Nectria* spores carried by the scale insects. The growth of the fungus in the cambium upsets normal bark formation, resulting in the pitting and cracking seen in the etching. With its bark damaged, the beech can no longer protect itself and becomes vulnerable to further infection by other parasitic, decay-producing fungi.

Beech snap

After secondary decay-producing fungi invade the damaged bark, carpenter ants move into the tree's rotting wood, where tunneling to create a home for the colony is easier. Long, vertical scars are then excavated by pileated woodpeckers foraging on the carpenter ants. Over a period of one or two decades, a predictable progression of organisms—scale insects, *Nectria* fungi, secondary wood-rot fungi, carpenter ants, pileated woodpeckers—eventually weaken a beech to the point of *beech snap*—where the tree's trunk actually snaps. As seen in the etching, this breaking of the trunk often occurs halfway between the forest floor and the tree's canopy, killing the trunk of the tree but leaving the root system intact. Prior to "snap," as the beech sickens, the tree sends up numerous root sprouts, a strategy that keeps the tree alive following the death of its main trunk. Often a dense thicket of young root sprouts surrounds older dying trees, as seen in the etching.

Examine the etching. Do you see any pattern to the bark damage on these infected beech? You may have noticed that bark cracking is more pronounced on one side of

BEECH SNAP

their trunks, a pattern commonly seen in beech with scale disease. Why is bark damage greater on one side of the trunk? Studies examining the colonization of newly infected trees show that the scale insects expand their coverage on the bark of beech by about one foot a year. The side of a tree first colonized develops a greater density of insects due to their limited mobility. The higher the density of insects, the more bark damage.

Trees resistant to the fungus do not display cracking bark. Instead, their trunks become covered with rounded knobs. Within these knobs the tree encapsulates the *Nectria* fungus and avoids the progression to beech snap by restricting the invasion of secondary wood-rot fungi. The healthy tree in this etching has probably survived because it is older and has thicker bark, too thick to be pierced by the stylet of the scale insect. As the remaining infected overstory beech succumb to "beech snap" and their young root sprouts grow to pole-sized trees about eight inches in diameter, the process of infection will be repeated. This time few, if any, trees will ever reach the stature of the old, central beech. Although beech will continue to be common in the forests of central New England due to its unsurpassed ability to root sprout, the seriousness of beech bark scale disease is such that the beech's presence as a dominant canopy tree in older forests will most likely be limited to high elevation sites.

A LOOK BACK

The introduction of forest pathogens has had a more profound impact on the forested landscape of central New England—and the entire deciduous forest of eastern North America, for that matter—than any other human activity. The beech scale insect and the *Nectria* fungus associated with it were one of the first accidentally introduced forest blights from Europe. The presence of the scale insect was discovered in forests around Halifax, Nova Scotia, in 1890. It is believed that the insect and fungus were borne on European beech logs shipped to North America.

Like the Native Americans who more than two hundred years earlier suffered from the accidental introduction of chicken pox, the American beech had no previous history of coevolution with the scale insect or fungus. Lacking appropriate adaptations, and defenseless against these foreign pathogens, it quickly succumbed to an ever-expanding blight that took a half century to migrate to central New England— reaching the region during World War II. By the mid-1970s, beech bark scale disease was killing beech trees as far as western New York and northern Pennsylvania.

Dutch elm disease

Although beech bark scale disease is probably the most easily observed forest blight in the region today, Dutch elm disease is the most commonly known, and also was accidentally introduced. In 1909, the first European elm bark beetle discovered in North America was found in Cambridge, Massachusetts. Once again, a shipment of logs from Europe was responsible for the introduction of the beetle and its commensalistic European fungus, *Ceratocystis ulmi*. The beetle lays its eggs under the bark of elm trees, and by itself—like the beech scale insect—does not present a real threat. However, if the beetle happens to carry spores of the *Ceratocystis* fungus and inoculates them while laying its eggs, the elm will yellow and eventually die. The fungus grows through the tree's vascular system, clogging it so that water and nutrients from the roots cannot reach the leaves, causing them to desiccate and die.

The first trees that succumbed to Dutch elm disease were identified in 1930 in Cleveland, Ohio. Within thirty years the blight had spread throughout the entire northeastern United States and stripped towns of their stately elm-lined streets. Early-nineteenth-century photographs of central New England towns usually show main streets shaded by a closed canopy of elms—in sharp contrast to their open appearance today. Keene, New Hampshire, was labeled the "Elm City" for its mile-long, elm-lined main street. Today less than a half-dozen large elms remain on Keene's main street, witnesses to the impact of Dutch elm disease.

Although the disappearance of this stately tree from New England's main streets and towns is a tragedy, the loss of this dramatic tree from rich-sited and floodplain forests where it grew had profound ecological ramifications. On certain riparian sites—floodplains and banks adjacent to rivers or streams—in both central and northern New England, American elms dominated forest canopies and sometimes reached heights of over one hundred feet. The interlacing, arching branches of these giant elms must have created forests with the feel of living cathedrals. Not one of these dramatic floodplain forests remains in all of New England.

Even though elm-dominated forests have disappeared, individual trees continue to survive and reproduce, providing hope that, in time, the American elm will develop resistance to the fungus and return to its former status. In fact, a disease-resistant strain called the Liberty elm has already been propagated by the Elm Research Institute in Harrisville, New Hampshire. By the year 2000 the institute anticipates that a million of these trees will have been planted in the eastern United States, possibly putting the elm well en route to recovery. However, there is a potential problem for the Liberty elm—all the trees are genetically identical, grafted from a single resistant tree. If a new American elm disease should develop to which the Liberty elm has no resistance, all of these one million trees will be at risk. The great hope of the Liberty elm is that it will reproduce with other native elms, passing its resistance to a more genetically diverse population of trees.

The American chestnut

Although both the beech and elm blights have affected forest composition in New England, they have not removed either species from the region's ecosystem. This is harder to say about the most tragic forest blight of all—the chestnut blight. The loss of the American chestnut was decisive, swift, and virtually complete.

It is believed that the Asian fungus *Cryphonectria parasitica* was accidentally introduced to North America on Chinese chestnut nursery stock and first started killing American chestnuts in 1904 at the Bronx Zoo. Spread by the native chestnut bark beetle, the fungus expanded its range at rates of up to fifty miles a year, and by 1950 more than 99.9 percent of all canopy chestnut trees throughout the species' range were dead. Unlike beech, which can root sprout when attacked by *Nectria* fungus, full-sized American chestnuts didn't stump-sprout when attacked by *Cryphonectria,* and as a result they died. Fortunately, nuts that were produced just before adult trees succumbed were able to germinate, and although the resulting trees were also attacked by the blight, they did have the ability to stump-sprout. Today, on warm sites in central New England and throughout southern New England, multiple-trunked, understory chestnuts are fairly common, the vast majority of them arising from root systems established by nuts that germinated at the onset of the blight.

The disastrous impact of this blight can be appreciated only when we understand the critical role the American chestnut played in the temperate deciduous forest of North America. The American chestnut was the most common forest tree east of the Mississippi, north of Georgia, and south of central New England. One out of four forest trees within this range was an American chestnut, and in the heart of its range—Tennessee and Kentucky—that number increased to one out of two. A truly majestic tree, it grew to diameters of ten feet and heights of 130 feet. Its nuts are still the most edible, to both humans and wildlife, of any nut-producing tree in North America. And the chestnut's wood is highly valued for its ability to be easily worked for furniture and dramatic rot resistance discussed in the previous chapter. (The rot-resistant quality of chestnut has allowed trees that succumbed to the blight over seventy years ago to remain as standing dead snags or fallen logs in the forests of the eastern United States.) In more ways than one, the American chestnut was the dominant tree of this country's deciduous forest biome.

But the dramatic impact of the chestnut blight is difficult to appreciate while exploring the woodlands of central New England. At the northern part of its range, the American chestnut was not as grand in size, nor as dominant in the canopy, as it was farther south. For me, it took a trip to Great Smoky Mountains National Park to

YOUNG STUMP-SPROUTED CHESTNUT

fully comprehend the blight's magnitude. While bushwhacking off a trail east of Gatlinburg, Tennessee, I came across what was once a mature stand of American chestnut. The dead chestnut snags had all been blown down and lay parallel on the ground covered in damp beds of moss and fern as much as a foot thick. The chestnut trunks averaged seven to eight feet in diameter and ran for more than eighty feet on the ground. Wandering through this woodland was like walking through a green maze. The only way to move was to walk along the side of a moss-covered trunk until I could cross its top, only to encounter another hulking, festooned giant. All about the downed chestnuts grew a forest of oaks averaging two to three feet in diameter. What would have been a majestic oak forest in central New England seemed a sorry replacement for the once grand chestnuts that lay on the ground.

Scattered throughout its range, including central New England, a few adult chestnuts have managed to survive the blight. The fungus kills trees by *girdling*—the destruction of the cambial tissue all the way around one section of the trunk, blocking the flow of water and nutrients—but the survivors seem to be able to encapsulate the fungus so that girdling doesn't occur. Nuts from these trees have been propagated and crossed with Chinese chestnuts in the hope of developing a resistant strain of American chestnut. The research is slow and lacks the initial success of the Liberty elm propagation program, but in time a resistant chestnut strain will most likely be developed. Unfortunately, due to the chestnut's inability to disperse its large nuts more than a couple of hundred feet, it may be an extremely long time, if ever, before this species regains prominence in the temperate deciduous forest region.

In the previous chapter I alluded to a disease that dramatically affected white pine in the first half of this century. Another Old World fungus, again accidentally introduced on nursery stock at the turn of the century, white pine blister rust devastated pine stands throughout central New England.

Blister rust, *Cronartium ribicola,* infects a tree when a fungal spore enters a *stomate*—a small opening for gas exchange—on a needle. The fungus grows through the vascular tissue, eventually killing the branch and working its way to the trunk. The pine's trunk develops oozing cankers that subsequently girdle the tree, causing death. Entire stands of white pine were lost to this fungus during the early 1900s. As a replacement to white-pine woodlands, red-pine plantations were planted throughout central New England between 1930 and 1960, red pine being unaffected by blister rust. All stands of red pine in New England are plantations of this vintage, unless they occur on dry, ledgy slopes—the native habitat of this species.

Today blister rust is more spotty in its distribution. To reproduce sexually, the blister rust fungus must parasitize currant—a berry-producing shrub—as well as white pine, but it can asexually reproduce on pine alone. Decades of effort to eradicate currant from central New England has resulted in reduced levels of white pine blister rust. Although blister rust does little damage to currant, to white pines the fungus is a killer; trees usually succumb within six years of infection.

Exotic insects

These four blights—beech bark scale disease, Dutch elm disease, chestnut blight, and white pine blister rust—are all caused by fungi, their spread often facilitated by insects. But in some introductions, insects alone are the problem. During the 1860s the European gypsy moth was brought to Massachusetts to be studied for its potential as a silk producer. Its escape from a laboratory initiated the first defoliation events witnessed in New England's forests.

Favoring oak-dominated woodlands, gypsy moth populations can explode with little warning, reducing canopy leaves to a shower of frass. A single defoliation rarely kills trees, unless they are conifers, which can't produce a new set of leaves once they are lost. But repeated defoliations, particularly on dry ridgetops and southern slopes where trees are more water-stressed, are often lethal.

The last major gypsy moth outbreak in central New England was during the summer of 1981. This outbreak gave rise to one of the most startling discoveries in the realm of plant ecology. It had long been known that plants are not helpless victims of munching insects. Although plants can't move, they can fight back with chemical weapons. Mechanical damage to their leaves causes some plants to increase the toxicity of their leaf tissues in order to render them unpalatable. What was discovered during research in the gypsy moth outbreak of 1981 was that oak trees not yet attacked by the gypsy moth larvae changed their leaf chemistry, apparently in anticipation of the approaching insects. Trees whose leaves were being consumed were somehow communicating this to their neighbors, who responded by increasing the toxicity of their leaves.

Two hypotheses were formulated to explain the phenomenon: Trees were communicating either through their grafted roots or through an airborne chemical message released from damaged leaves. Research proved the latter hypothesis to be correct. (The chemical message was discovered to be jasmonic acid.)

Why would trees evolve to alert their neighbors to the presence of defoliating insects? Wouldn't it be more advantageous for a tree to have an unsuspecting neighbor defoliated and thus be released from competition for sunlight? That might be a plausible strategy if just a few trees are defoliated, but insects like the gypsy moth can irrupt to astounding numbers. After the leaves of surrounding neighbors have been eaten, the remaining trees have to protect themselves from a growing army of leaf-eaters. As with many species, the best defense is unity.

Defoliation events are controlled by the general vigor and health of forest trees. When trees have been weakened by drought or other environmental factors, similar to the way stress can weaken a person's immune system, they are slow to respond to the presence of gypsy moth larvae. If they cannot mobilize their chemical arsenals, the gypsy moth population flourishes, and defoliation follows. Luckily, repeated annual defoliations are rare, meaning the impact of the gypsy moth, though more dramatic in appearance, is less than the often lethal fungal blights discussed before.

At the doorstep of central New England awaits another insect defoliator. Accidentally introduced from Asia and first discovered in Pennsylvania in the 1960s, the woolly adelgid has spread as far north as southern Massachusetts. Its tolerance to cold temperatures has researchers worried about the future of its host, the eastern hemlock.

The adelgid is quite similar to the beech scale insect. It is minute, protects itself in a white, waxy covering, and sucks the hemlock's sap. Rather than attacking bark on the trunk, the adelgid is attracted to the bark of twigs supporting needles. In dense populations it can cause the wilting of branches and, within a few years, the death of the tree. Once attacked by the adelgid, no hemlock has been known to survive. Although Vermont, New Hampshire, and Maine have quarantined hemlock logs and nursery stock from parts south since 1988, the adelgid will most likely expand northward. Carried by birds, deer, and human activity, it is just a matter of time before central New England will have yet another introduced forest pathogen. To make matters worse, the potential impact of this introduced insect to New England forests clearly dwarfs that of the gypsy moth, which rarely kills trees.

WOOLLY ADELGID ON HEMLOCK TWIG

Forest health

The list of New England's exotic forest pathogens discussed in this chapter is by no means complete. It only highlights some of the most visibly affected tree species. To a forest ecologist it is not the impact these pathogens have on trees that is of primary concern, but rather their effect on the health of the entire forest ecosystem. Just as doctors use blood pressure and pulse rates to monitor human health, ecologists use three main diagnostics to measure declining ecosystem health. They are: a decrease in the rate of photosynthesis within the ecosystem, an increase in the rate of nutrient loss from the ecosystem, and decreases in biodiversity over short periods of time.

As forests and other ecosystems mature, their trees and plants grow larger and support more total surface area in their leaves. This means that maturing ecosystems increase the rate at which photosynthesis occurs. At the same time, the root systems of the plants grow more extensive, as does the network of fungal *mycelia*—microscopic root-like threads that intertwine through the soil. The developing roots and mycelium increase the nutrient absorbing efficiency of the ecosystem, holding nutrients that would otherwise be leached from the soil and carried away by the movement of groundwater. The number of species in an ecosystem slowly changes through time; however, it does not always increase as an ecosystem matures. A maturing forest that comes to be dominated by hemlock usually experiences a decline in biodiversity due to the deep shade and acidic soils that hemlock produce. Yet this decline is gradual, occurring over a period of decades. A rapid decline in biodiversity is a sign of ecosystem illness.

Forest blights negatively impact all three of these processes. Defoliation greatly reduces the forest's ability to conduct photosynthesis. With fewer canopy leaves, less solar energy is collected for the process of photosynthesis and more reaches and warms the forest floor. The warming of the forest floor increases rates of decomposition, a process that releases nutrients. When photosynthesis drops and decomposition increases, the loss of nutrients from the system is accelerated; more nutrients become available, but fewer are being taken up by plants because rates of nutrient uptake are directly related to rates of photosynthesis. Because trees interact with countless other organisms, such as insects, fungi, and vertebrates, the loss of a tree species from a forest will most likely result in the loss of other species in close association with that tree. We don't know if species of fungi or insects were extinguished by the chestnut blight, but it is possible that some were. If beeches are reduced to understory trees and produce few nuts, what will be the impact on turkey, squirrel, and bear? Bear rely heavily on beechnuts in central and northern New England to produce winter fat for hibernation, and with their numbers already in decline from habitat loss, the beech blight is not good news.

We can't say for certain how the loss of a particular tree species will affect a forest, but a general rule of ecology states that the extirpation of species from an ecosystem will move that ecosystem toward instability. The more species removed, the less stable the system becomes. When the species being removed are canopy dominants that exert a strong influence on the forest ecosystem, we have good reason to be concerned.

Luckily, our New England forests continue to display resiliency in response to introduced pathogens. We have not witnessed the level of widespread ecosystem decline that can be seen in parts of Germany's Black Forest region, where one out of every two trees is a standing dead snag. Yet the resiliency of the New England forest is certainly not what it was prior to these accidental introductions. We could compare our forests to an individual with an immune system that is not working at full potential. Because of that, we need to be concerned about other, human-induced stressors to our forested landscape. We will examine some of these stressors in chapter 8.

Whenever I encounter a large, healthy beech, discover a one-foot-diameter chestnut, or see a stately elm silhouetted against a pastoral landscape, I am inspired, but not comforted. They are reminders of the losses suffered by our New England forests. Some of the losses may be recovered, the American elm being an example. Others, like the American chestnut, may never return to their rightful status. And in the case of the hemlock, we can't even predict what the extent of the loss will be. Our forests are different from how they were prior to European settlement, but unlike the more temporary changes produced by the clear-cutting of forest for pasture or the development of twentieth-century logging practices, the changes wrought by introduced forest pathogens will remain for thousands of years to come.

chapter five
ABANDONMENT

From my house, a ten-minute walk takes me through a young pine woods to the crest of a high, open meadow, then down into a valley that supports the most extensive beaver ponds within the range of my wanderings. Two large ponds form the heart of the area, the bigger pond lying farther back at the base of the rugged, aptly named Rocky Ridge. Beavers have inhabited this once forested valley for over three decades, moving alternately from one pond to the other. Because of its wild appearance, created by hundreds of standing dead snags, the area is an all-season magnet for my explorations.

Although only a few minutes from my home, the ponds, particularly the farther one, create the strongest sense of wilderness that I have encountered in the region. Standing on skis at midnight, alone under a January full moon, surrounded by large spruce and pine snags, my feeling of seclusion is as great as any I've ever experienced. Yet this is far from an untouched environment. It is a highly manipulated ecosystem, one that has been dramatically altered to suit the needs of a single species—the beaver. Beavers are the only animals, other than humans, that will create entirely new ecosystems for their own use. And often, like humans, once they have depleted an area's resources, they will abandon their holdings and move on.

The etching at the beginning of this chapter does not depict one of the ponds near my home, but it does show an abandoned beaver pond, a common sight in central New England. How can we tell that this pond is abandoned? How long ago did the beaver leave this pond? What was the quality of the habitat for the beavers when they created the pond? These questions are the focus of this chapter; however, before we attempt to find the answers, we need more information on the life history of the beaver.

Beavers flood forests and create ponds for two reasons. The first is safety. Slow on land, especially in snow, beavers are easy prey for large predators, but in the sanctity of a pond, they are almost completely free from predation. The second is that ponds foster the development of their summertime food supply. Aquatic plants like water lilies, pickerelweed, and cattails are common summer staples. During the winter their diet shifts to the bark of trees. If they are successful in storing a large enough supply of limbs in their pond during the fall, they may never need to leave the protected confines of their watery home for an entire winter season.

CONCAVE FORM OF BEAVER DAM

The dams beavers construct to create their ponds are composed of a combination of sticks and mud. Although they can deplete the trees around their ponds, these animals are true conservationists when it comes to recycling. All of the sticks, whose bark supported the beavers through the winter, are reused to build the dam and lodge. A truly impressive dam can reach a height of over ten feet. At this dimension the dam often takes on a concave form, bowing into the pond and gaining added strength from its horizontal, archlike structure. When I first moved to Vermont, I came upon an impressive dam like this one in the town of Dummerston. The downstream side was a vaulted nest of smooth gray sticks that rose to meet the pond's surface at the very top of the dam. The dam spanned forty feet, and from its base—in the former streambed—it rose eleven feet.

Odds are that if you encounter a beaver pond, it will be abandoned like the one in the etching. Most beavers will inhabit a pond for only five to twenty years, but abandoned ponds can last for many decades. Because beavers invest both time and energy in the construction of their dam and lodge, why would they choose to leave the pond? The chief reason for abandonment is a depleted winter food supply. Because beavers are more susceptible to predation on land, they rarely travel more than two hundred feet from their pond margin. In marshy areas they dig canals that radiate from the pond's perimeter to gain access to more distant woodlands. But once all their preferred species of trees have been cut and consumed within a couple of hundred feet of the pond margin or canal terminus, beavers will abandon the pond in favor of a new home.

Beavers have a distinct hierarchy among the species of trees they harvest for winter food. Most preferred in central New England are members of the willow family, including aspens and the cottonwood, all of which have bark that is easily digestible and high in protein. Next come the oaks and ashes, followed by sugar maple. Members of the rose family, such as apples and cherries, are also important. Of moderate interest are members of the birch family, especially musclewood, black birch, and paper birch. Gray birch, yellow birch, speckled alder, hop hornbeam, beech, and red maple are low on the beaver's food preference list, and conifers like pine and hemlock lie at the very bottom. When we see conifers being cut and their bark consumed, it is a sign that the beavers will likely be abandoning the pond within a year's passing. (This, however, should not be confused with girdling activity. To encourage the growth of their preferred trees, beavers often girdle and kill young pines and hemlock. Girdled trees are never felled; they have their bark removed all the way around the base with little evidence that the wood has been chewed.)

Beavers have preferences not only for certain species, but for trees of certain sizes, as well. Imagine yourself a beaver: What size trees would you seek to fell, cut up into manageable lengths, and haul back to the pond? From the perspective of a beaver, pole-sized trees, those four to six inches in diameter, provide a better food supply than either larger or smaller trees. This is because the amount of bark offered by a pole-sized tree, relative to the beaver's energy expenditure in cutting and hauling it, makes it the best choice. A beaver's dreamscape would be a forest of pole-sized aspens; its nightmare, a stand of mature hemlocks.

The composition of the surrounding forest will determine how long a beaver pond will be active, but the pond's topographic setting is important, too. Given two ponds surrounded by similar forests, which type of topographic setting will support an active beaver pond for a longer period of time, one sited in a broad, flat valley or one that lies in a narrow ravine? Each year, as beavers cut more trees, they use the debarked limbs to increase the height of their dam. This causes the pond to expand the area of its coverage. In a broad valley, as trees are depleted around the pond, increasing the dam height by only a foot may flood the denuded forest and extend the two-hundred-foot zone to new harvestable trees. Increasing dam height in a ravine, on the

GIRDLED HEMLOCK

other hand, will do little to enlarge the pond and thus will not increase access to new trees. All things being the same, beaver ponds in broad, flat valleys are active for longer periods of time.

As previously mentioned, the pond in the etching that precedes this chapter is abandoned. From the evidence at hand, how can this be surmised? Can we tell how many years ago the beaver left? Is it possible to assess the quality of the pond's original habitat for beaver to develop a rough estimate of how long the pond was inhabited? The etching holds the answers to all these questions.

Dating abandonment

The very first sign that beavers are no longer in residence can be observed about two weeks after their leaving. The water level in the pond will drop one-half to one foot. Without the beavers' daily attention to the dam, numerous leaks develop. Unless there is a drought, an active pond maintains its water level right at the top of the dam.

When beavers emerge from their lodge to begin their nocturnal activities, the first order of business is to examine the dam. Their inspection is auditory in nature. If the noise of running water is low, a little bit of mudding on the pond side of the dam may be in order. Beavers scoop mud from the pond bottom and carry it between their chin and forelegs to be used to patch small leaks. (Contrary to cartoon impersonations, their tails play no role in mudding. The major use of the tail is for fat storage, which helps carry beavers through long winters.) But if beavers hear the sound of rushing water, dam-building activity is stimulated. It is such a strong

STUMPS IN FOREGROUND

TURKEY TAILS

stimulus that researchers have been able to get beavers to build dams on dry land in response to the sound of rushing water on a tape recorder. Without this nightly repair work, the pond's water level begins to drop.

The lowered water exposes the rich moist mud on the pond side of the dam. During the growing season it takes only about one to two months for this area to become vegetated with herbaceous plants. Since the stream side of the dam is not mudded, little herbaceous growth will occur on an active dam; however, this side may support shrubs on older, maintained dams. The pond in the etching displays a lowered water level and herbaceous growth on the pond side of the dam. Does this suggest that it has been abandoned only for a couple of months?

There is other evidence that points to a longer period of vacancy. The stumps left by beaver activity are the next detail to examine when dating beaver pond abandonment. A tree that has been cut within one year's time leaves a stump with blond-colored wood. Numerous blond-colored stumps surrounding an abandoned pond date the beavers' departure at less than a year. If there are just a couple of these stumps, it is most likely the result of another beaver wandering through in search of suitable habitat following the pond's abandonment. The foreground of the etching shows two stumps, neither of which is blond.

Of these two stumps, one has gray wood, which dates its cutting to more than a year ago; the other supports the growth of turkey tails, a species of shelf fungus that grows on decaying wood and is never visible on stumps less than three years old. Without any other evidence at hand, we would need to walk around the pond examining stumps and age the pond's abandonment based on the proportion of blond to gray to turkey tailed. If few blond stumps were found and most were gray and turkey tail–free, we'd guess one to three years had passed since the beavers' departure. If few stumps were free of turkey tails, we'd guess more than three years had passed. Luckily, there is one more piece of evidence in the etching that will allow us to put a more definitive date on abandonment.

In chapter 3, I mentioned that the bark that forms on hemlock wounds shows visible annual growth lines. Any wound on a hemlock, whether from the rubbing of a stag's antlers during rutting season or from the gnawing of a beaver whose preferred winter food supply has been exhausted, can be accurately dated. The hemlock on the right-hand side of the etching clearly displays three growth lines in the bark surrounding a beaver gnawing. This hemlock was not girdled, but sampled as a possible food tree. We can surmise this because the bark was not cut all the way around the hemlock and some of the wood was gnawed. When beavers start sampling hemlocks in this fashion, it is a sure sign that they are having a difficult time finding enough trees to supply their winter needs. In this case, it is also strong evidence that this pond was abandoned two to three years ago due to a depleted supply of winter trees.

HEMLOCK SHOWING WOUND AND BARK GROWTH RINGS

Now that we have a sense of when the pond was abandoned, let's turn our questions to the quality of habitat when the beavers arrived. The pond is surrounded by conifers. Does this suggest that the original quality of habitat for the beavers was poor, since their preferred species of trees are missing? Not necessarily, for a coniferous border, like the one in the etching, is a fairly common feature of old or abandoned ponds. The cutting of hardwoods and the recutting of their stump-sprouts eventually leave the residual pines and hemlocks and their seedlings to flourish in openings, free from hardwood competition, creating a band of conifers that surrounds

CONIFEROUS BORDER OF POND

the pond. So how can we assess the quality of habitat at the time when beavers first invaded the area? The answer lies in the pond's standing dead snags.

Because flooding, and the associated lack of oxygen, keeps the roots of dead trees from rotting, beaver pond snags will stand for decades following abandonment. The etching shows few snags emerging from the pond. If the area was originally forest, what does this suggest? It indicates that most of the trees were cut by the beavers and that, therefore, the original forest was probably composed of preferred species. This, in turn, suggests that the beavers inhabited this pond for a good number of years, as the area supported an ample winter food supply. A pond with numerous standing dead snags suggests that the original forest was dominated by conifers or yellow birch, trees rarely felled by beavers.

POND WITH SNAGS

Beavers begin their search for new ponds in the spring. Not only do adults abandon old ponds at this time, but also all two-year-old kits are chased out of their family ponds by their parents to search for their own places of residence. Because beavers have annual broods, forcing out the two-year-olds is necessary to make room for the young. A two-year apprenticeship is enough for a young beaver to learn all the skills involved in tree felling, hauling, dam and lodge construction, and canal making. Beavers don't reach reproductive age until their third year, which slows population growth rates for the species. This is an unusual strategy in the rodent family, but one that makes sense for an animal with such large resource needs and complex skills development.

Beavers begin their search for a new home by moving up or down the watershed. Ponds already established by beavers have *scent posts*—piles of leaves, mud, and small sticks—on which the animals leave their scent to alert newcomers that the pond is inhabited. If one of the pond's mated pair has died, the scent post announces the vacancy through the absence of one gender's scent. If the newcomer happens to be of the "vacant" gender, he or she will move in to complete the monogamous pairing.

If beavers find no suitable habitat in their own watershed, they migrate to new watersheds. This usually involves some significant travel on land, making this the most dangerous period of a beaver's life. More dead beavers are seen on roadsides in April and May than at any other time of year—the majority of them two-year-olds in search of new homes.

Changes in old ponds

Once a pond is abandoned, it undergoes changes in vegetation. The condition of the dam is primarily responsible for influencing the successional outcomes. If the dam is strong and continues to hold water, the pond will evolve—as it continues to fill with stream-borne sediment—toward a marsh or "beaver meadow," a wetland dominated by sedges, rushes, and cattails. In time, as decaying plant material builds up in the marsh, wetland shrubs like willows, alders, dogwoods, and viburnums find acceptable sites for germination and convert the marsh into a shrubby swamp. Through the annual decay of their leaves, shrubs add to the buildup of organic matter in the wetland, eventually creating conditions dry enough for trees to establish themselves. Red maple is very tolerant of saturated substrates and often dominates wetlands that have developed to this stage. Given enough time, the swamp may fill and dry to the point that a wet-sited forest develops.

BEAVER SCENT POST

If the dam is breached and the pond drains, a forest can develop much more quickly. Grasses and other herbaceous plants will first colonize the rich, exposed sediments of the pond bottom. But trees may move in quickly. Depending on the seed source from surrounding trees or a coinciding mast year for a particular species, the composition of the drained pond's future forest could be almost anything. Whichever route succession takes, either through a progression of wetlands or through more direct forest establishment, in some period of time a winter food supply for beavers will be regenerated, and the process of beaver impoundment will start all over again, in some cases with a new dam being built directly on the site of an old one.

This cyclic pattern of successional change created by beaver activity adds a wonderfully diverse mosaic to any landscape in which these creatures are found. Without beaver impoundments—in all states of activity and abandonment—our regional ecosystem would be impoverished. Although beavers do deplete their local resources and move on, the depletion is temporary and results in a parade of varied ecosystems that create critical habitat for numerous species of plants and wildlife. So the next time you encounter an abandoned beaver meadow, don't be afraid to get your feet wet. Walk in and contemplate the fact that beneath you lie deposits, layer upon layer, from the beaver ponds that have cycled there through the millennia.

A LOOK BACK

Although beavers have been an important component of the central New England landscape for thousands of years, less than a century ago it was impossible to find one active impoundment in the region. Trapping to provide furs for European hat markets led to the beavers' extermination by the early 1800s. With the exception of northern Maine, where some were spared, all of New England's beavers were eliminated in less than two centuries.

Beaver trapping in central New England, a major component of the fur trade with the British, began with the establishment of William Pynchon's trading post in Springfield, Massachusetts, in 1636. This post served as the major clearinghouse for furs throughout central New England. Ironically, the development of commercial trapping, and the ultimate extirpation of the beaver, was directly related to the decline of another New England population. The epidemics that decimated Native peoples created conditions that made a commercial fur trade viable by tearing great holes in the social fabric of tribal culture.

Prior to the introduction of European diseases, tribal leadership developed in orderly ways, often through lineage. The epidemics changed this orderly progression. Tribes were broken, scattered, and constantly reconfigured as illness wiped out village after village. Ascension to leadership positions was no longer based solely on an individual's record of service to the tribe. Individuals who were ascribed as carrying prestige filled leadership roles, and the British created conditions where prestige did not have to be earned; it could be traded for. It could be gained in the form of *wampum*.

Wampum consisted of colored, cylindrical beads fashioned from the shells of whelks and quahogs. They were highly revered by Native people, and they were usually worn in very modest amounts, only by people of high status. The use of wampum by the British as currency, during a period of profoundly unstable tribal life, spawned a fur trade of great proportions. Among Native people, what had once been self-reliant trapping of furbearers for indigenous use became market trapping for wampum and the heightened prestige that it brought.

Beavers were the preferred prey due to their sedentary nature and the high value the British placed on their pelts. The ease with which trappers could find their lodges, and the beavers' predictable behavior, made them the most easily trapped of all furbearers. With their low reproductive rates, it is not surprising that the number of beavers trapped in central New England had dropped precipitously by 1670. By 1700, trade in beaver pelts was almost nonexistent. During the eighteenth century, the last remnants of the beaver were swept from the region, to be found only in the northern reaches of Maine, New Hampshire, and Vermont. Extermination from the latter two states occurred by 1850.

The reintroduction of the beaver to central New England was just as rapid as its extirpation. First occurring in southern Vermont in 1921, by 1940 beavers had established populations in all central New England states. In the last half century, beavers have vigorously reclaimed their territory throughout New England. This is truly a story of success for the well-being of our regional landscape, because beaver activity fosters biodiversity through the array of habitats it creates.

Yet the removal and associated reintroduction of beavers were not free of short-term, negative side effects. By the middle of the nineteenth century, farm abandonment was at record rates. Lowland areas that formerly had been in cultivation, used as mowings, or pasture, were let go. Other lowland areas that had not been cleared also underwent successional processes in the absence of beavers. At the point of their reintroduction, beavers found ample forest habitat, much of it the same successional age. With freedom from trapping and the absence of large predators, they quickly expanded their population in the region and began to exploit their regional habitat in a synchronized fashion, meaning that at some time in the future, most of their habitat would be in the same degraded state.

In my explorations of southeastern Vermont and southwestern New Hampshire, beaver habitat with a winter food supply that can support an active colony for many years is hard to find. The vast majority of it has already been utilized by beavers and abandoned, and I have great difficulty finding impoundments that have been active for more than just a few years. I have also seen new ponds being established late in the summer and sometimes even early fall, an indication that beavers are needing to search far longer for future homes. Often these new impoundments are developed in the most marginal areas in terms of winter food supply. It is evidence of a last-ditch stand after a long summer of searching with no success. The residents of such sites rarely make it through the winter before succumbing to starvation. On a positive note, I am convinced that this situation is merely a small blip and that, in time, asynchrony will again develop in the grand cycle of beaver impoundment and abandonment.

The beaver should be revered as the creator of a landscape mosaic—a rich assortment of varied wetland ecosystems. No other creature fashions such an array of habitats on which so many other species are dependent. How poor our countryside would become if this species were again to be lost. Thankfully, unless humans again interfere, beavers are sure to remain an important component of our New England landscape.

chapter six
PILLOWS AND CRADLES

Geographically, the heart of central New England is the southwestern corner of New Hampshire. Within this region lies New England's second largest state park. Pisgah State Park covers thirteen thousand acres of ledgy ridges dissected by numerous lakes, ponds, and wetlands. Because of the rugged terrain, a large portion of its forest was never cleared for agriculture and contained some of the last pockets of old-growth white pine in central New England. The etching at the end of chapter 3 is modeled after a 1915 photograph taken in Pisgah, and the size of the white pine in the etching is not exaggerated. Even though the large pines no longer exist, Pisgah remains a wonderful representation of central New England's forested landscape.

The forest depicted in the etching on the facing page is just one of the numerous hemlock-dominated stands found in Pisgah. Although it looks similar to many hemlock forests, it displays a feature absent from the etching of the hemlock forest at the beginning of chapter 3. Can you see the differentiating feature? The ground under these hemlocks is highly irregular; its numerous mounds almost give a sense of movement to the forest floor. These mounds and what they tell us about the history of this forest are the focus of this chapter.

What created the mounds? Are they the result of human activity? What are they composed of—rock or soil? When numerous mounds are encountered in New England forests, they usually are not the result of human activity, but rather a consequence of the action of water, wind, or ice.

Water always migrates downhill and pools in low spots, sometimes just below the ground's surface. When a permanently high water table develops in this way, trees growing on such a site have to contend with a special problem. Oxygen normally diffuses from the air into small pores in the soil, but if these pores are filled with water, only small amounts of oxygen can enter the soil and become available for tree roots. Without sufficient oxygen, the roots can't grow.

A tree's response, in this case, is to grow roots very close to the surface, where the supply of oxygen is greater. If the soil is saturated all the way to the surface, trees will be found only on raised mounds called *hummocks*—a familiar sight to people who frequent swamps. Hummocks first form when trees germinate on downed logs, stumps, or the raised root systems of other woody plants. The roots of the growing tree slowly replace the original material and eventually create a hummock composed of the roots clustered in a mound under its trunk but above the water table. When we first bought land in southeastern Vermont, my wife, Marcia, asked why all the trees in one section of our pine forest were growing on mounds. Up to that point I hadn't noticed what she had, nor that sinuous pine roots laced the ground's surface. I now know that this is a site with a very high water table where pines can survive only on hummocks, the depressions between the hummocks being perennially wet.

As numerous trees in the etching are not growing on raised mounds, we must look for clues other than a high water table to explain the irregular surface topography.

Between thirteen thousand and fourteen thousand years ago, a southern portion of the Laurentide Ice Sheet, which had covered New England for thousands of years, melted away and retreated northward into Quebec. Trapped within its ice were hordes of large rocks and boulders that had been plucked from the region's mountains and cliffs when the glacier was slowly expanding southward. With the melting of the ice, the boulders were dropped in place, their aggregate tracing a path back to their site of origin. The trails these rocks create across the countryside are called "boulder trains" and can stretch for miles. After centuries of moss growth and the buildup of forest litter, some of these rocks become hard to identify as boulders, and as earth-covered mounds, they often support full-sized trees. Some of the mounds in the etching are topped by black birch, recognized by the horizontal lines in its dark bark. But there is evidence suggesting that these mounds are not glacially transported boulders.

MOUND AND DEPRESSION

A closer look reveals that a depression lies to the right of each mound. Glacial boulders would not consistently have depressions associated with them in this fashion. The close association of depression and mound hints that the mounds could be composed of material that was excavated from the depressions. Would people dig a series of holes like this? Probably not. If the mounds are not the result of a high water table, glacially transported boulders, or human activity, what could have created them? The only remaining answer is that the mounds must be the result of wind.

This "pit and mound" or, as Neil Jorgensen calls it, "pillow and cradle" topography is the result of a *blowdown*. A blowdown is a wind event strong enough to topple and uproot live trees. As a tree is blown over, its roots are ripped from the ground carrying a large amount of earth. This removal of roots and earth excavates a pit, or "cradle." Within a few decades, the roots decay and drop the excavated earth next to the depression, creating the mound, or "pillow." By standing on a pillow and looking directly over its cradle, we are facing the direction from which the wind came. From the orientation of the pillows and cradles in this hemlock forest, the wind blew from the lower right to the upper left and uprooted several trees.

UPROOTED TREE

Direction of fall

With the exception of tornadoes, all blowdowns share a common feature: They topple trees so that they all lie facing the same general direction. The powerful cyclonic flow of a tornado can down trees in all directions, but in central New England tornadoes are rare—our irregular, hilly topography disrupts the formation of highly organized, cyclonic winds. When trees are seen lying in all directions, it is usually the result of *deadfall*—standing, dead trees felled at different times by winds from various directions.

It is easy to separate deadfall from the impact of a tornado. When dead snags fall, their decayed roots usually excavate little earth, creating small pillows and cradles (notice the fallen snag in chapter 1's etching). Tornadoes will also leave numerous trees, particularly pines, snapped at midtrunk height. Cyclonic winds don't push a tree in one direction, so the roots remain planted while a tornado's extreme rotational torque literally rips off trees' tops.

Once you develop an eye for discerning pillows and cradles, you will observe them frequently throughout New England. Yet from the evidence at hand, is it possible to do more than simply deduct that a blowdown has occurred? You can sometimes date the wind event by season or even by year. Even if the trees have completely decayed, you can guess if the uprooted trees were conifers or hardwoods and infer the composition of the original forest. Learning to read a blowdown allows you to gain a deeper understanding of the history of a particular forested landscape.

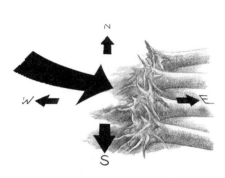

WIND PATTERN OF SUMMER STORM

Determining the time of year a blowdown occurred is possible because the direction of windfall is usually consistent by season. During the spring and summer, the strongest winds are generated by *thunderstorm microbursts*—concentrated, downward bursts of wind that hit the landscape and then radiate out in a semicircular pattern. Since the winds of a thunderstorm come from the west, the path of microbursts is from the west as well, but upon hitting the ground they radiate out and topple trees so that the downed trunks form an arc pointing from the northeast to the southeast. If you measure all the directions the downed trunks point and take the average, it will be close to due east, confirming that the wind came from the west. Trees uprooted in an easterly direction are the hallmark of a severe thunderstorm, and even if they have decayed, their pillows and cradles will record it.

On the morning of July 15, 1995, a powerful, well-organized line of thunderstorms developed in New York State. Within three hours, they leveled thousands of acres in

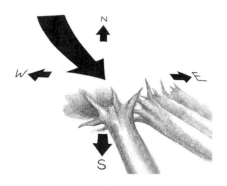

WIND PATTERN OF WINTER GALE

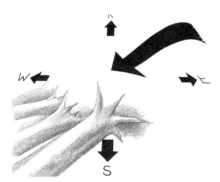

WIND PATTERN OF NORTHEASTER

the Adirondacks and swept through just about all of central New England. Millions of trees were uprooted or snapped in half by this single frontal system. On our property in Westminster, Vermont, twenty large white pines were uprooted, and many others were snapped at midtrunk height. All of the snapped and uprooted trees lay on the ground, their tops radiating in an arc that pointed from twenty degrees north of east to thirty degrees south of east. The neighboring trees on either side sustained much lighter damage, mostly in the form of broken branches. It appears that our property was the recipient of a thunderstorm microburst.

Trees that fall in a southeasterly to southerly direction are usually the result of strong high-pressure gales associated with fall and winter arctic air masses blowing in from the northwest. Any trees that fall toward the western side of a north–south axis are the victims of either winter northeasters or summer/fall hurricanes, both being strong cyclonic storms with a counterclockwise rotation. Northeasters are so named because their winds come predominantly from that direction, so any trees they topple fall in a westerly to southerly direction. The direction that trees are felled by a hurricane is related to their position with respect to the storm's path. Trees in forests to the east of a hurricane are toppled to the northwest by strong southeasterly winds. Trees on the western side of a hurricane fall to the southwest because the strongest winds they experience come from the northeast. Trees downed to the northwest are clear evidence of a hurricane; trees downed to the southwest are victims of either a hurricane or a winter northeaster.

When we peer straight into the etching, we are looking due north, so the west is to our left and the east to our right. Examine again the arrangement of the pillows and their associated cradles. Based on their orientation, from which direction did the winds come that caused this blowdown? During what season did this event most likely occur, and what kind of storm was it?

We can discount thunderstorms with strong winds from the west or winter storms with winds from either the northwest or northeast. The winds that generated this blowdown came from the southeast and toppled trees toward the northwest. Only a hurricane with the center of its path to the west of Pisgah State Park would down trees toward the northwest.

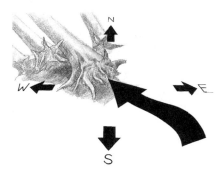

WIND PATTERN OF HURRICANE

The date of the storm

Now that we have identified the cause of the blowdown as a hurricane, can we date it to a specific year? Because hurricanes that cause blowdowns in central New England are infrequent, occurring at an average rate of one per century, we can have some success dating the pit-and-mound topography created by them. To date the year of the etching's hurricane, we need to examine the trees growing on the pillows.

Once a tree is uprooted, the exposed earth in its root mass becomes a good site for the successful germination of seeds that need to contact litter-free soil. This is a common requirement for trees with very small seeds like birches, aspens, and pines. Having very limited stored-energy reserves, roots from these germinating seeds need to establish quickly. Unlike larger oak or maple seeds, with energy reserves that allow them time to push roots through extensive litter, seeds of birches, aspens, and pines will perish on a bed of leaves and duff.

BIRCH ON MOUND

HEMLOCK NOT ON MOUND

Not only does the downed tree create a good germination site for small-seeded trees, but it also creates a gap in the canopy, allowing a dramatic increase in sunlight. The forest's response is quick; the trees most effective at taking advantage of this opportunity are often birches, whose seeds annually carpet the forest floor. The sixteen-inch black birches on the pillows in the etching are most likely between forty and seventy years of age. The only hurricane to create extensive blowdowns in central New England during this time frame struck September 21, 1938.

One of the most dramatic forested sites I have visited that was affected by the "Great Hurricane of 1938" is a very steep, southeast-facing slope close to the Connecticut River in Springfield, Vermont. The forest is dominated by old white oaks, most of which have trunks growing roughly at a forty-five-degree angle and pointing directly to the northwest. Their unusual growth is the result of hurricane winds that only partially uprooted them; their strong canopy limbs braced against the steep slope kept them from falling completely. All remain healthy to this day, frozen in place from an event that occurred over a half century ago.

Let's go further in our examination of the etching and see if we can find clues that will give us some information about the composition of the original forest prior to the 1938 hurricane. Because most of the hemlocks in the etching are slightly larger than the black birches and are not found growing on the pillows, it is a good guess that they were already established in the understory at the time of the hurricane. Other evidence in the etching will also tell us that some of the uprooted trees were conifers, most likely hemlock or white pine.

Nurse logs

In chapter 3 we compared the decay patterns of conifers and hardwoods. We will now add another dimension to the process of wood decay—the development of moss beds on rotting logs. As you may recall, downed trunks of maples, beeches, and birches decay quickly, usually at a rate too fast for a coating of moss to develop, while the rot-resistant sapwood of oaks and chestnuts restricts its growth. It is the trunks of conifers, rotting slowly from the outside in, that most often become moss covered. Small seeds of birches, pines, and hemlocks lodge in the moss covering of decaying conifer logs, which create wonderful germination sites. A downed, moss-covered log on which numerous trees germinate and successfully grow is called a *nurse log*. Can you find evidence of a nurse log in the etching?

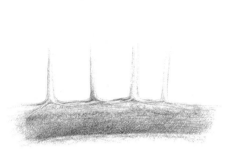

NURSE LOG

Whenever trees grow in a line, with aboveground, interlacing roots tracing that line, it is a clear sign that they established on a nurse log that has since rotted away. The line of smaller hemlocks on the left-hand side of the etching is evidence of a former nurse log, most likely a hemlock or white pine. Although nurse logs are a common phenomenon in the Pacific Northwest due to the abundance of large conifers, in central New England we usually see evidence of nurse logs only where hemlocks are found growing. Since the development of a moss bed on a nurse log often takes a couple of decades, providing ample time for a young forest to establish a dense canopy over the nurse log, only shade-tolerant trees can colonize them. Hemlock and yellow birch are the sole shade-tolerant, small-seeded trees in central New England. Of the two, hemlock can grow in far deeper shade. In fact, hemlock has the greatest tolerance for shade of all trees in the region. That high shade tolerance and its success for germinating in moss make the hemlock the most common proprietor of the region's nurse logs.

The presence of a nurse log, which was created by the blowdown, implies that some of the canopy trees in this forest prior to 1938 were either hemlock or white pine. The toppled conifers were probably less than two feet in diameter because really large hemlocks or pines would not have completely rotted away in less than sixty years. In many sites throughout the region, the decaying remains of big conifers dropped by the hurricane of '38 are still visible—their rot-resistant limbs poking through beds of moss that lie on surprisingly sound heartwood.

In summary, from the etching we can read that just prior to 1938 the forest canopy was dominated by trees not much larger than two feet in diameter, some of which were conifers, standing over an understory of hemlock. The canopy trees were leveled by the 1938 hurricane, which released the understory hemlock to become the new canopy dominants. Black birch established on the pillows and hemlock colonized the nurse log.

The pillows and cradles in this forest are pronounced and readily noticeable, but on some sites, the blowdown of big trees doesn't create observable pits or mounds. On ledgy outcrops with thin soils, a downed tree will leave only subtle signs of pillows and cradles because little soil clings to the roots. The same is true in sandy substrates, where the roots simply pop out of the ground. Evidence of blowdowns on ledgy or sandy sites may last for several decades; however, on those sites that display prominent pillow-and-cradle topography, it will be a long-term exhibition. These irregularities in the forest floor last for many hundreds of years. Along with stone walls, pillows and cradles have great longevity and remain as guides to help us decipher the history of the forested landscape.

A LOOK BACK

The Great Hurricane of 1938 began on September 4 as a barely noticeable upper-air depression—the origin of a low-pressure weather system—in the south-central region of the Sahara desert. At that time, no one could have predicted that in less than three weeks the depression would grow into a deadly hurricane that would cross the Atlantic Ocean and first strike land on Long Island, New York.

The very first knowledge of the hurricane's existence came from a ship—the SS *Algegrete*—sailing northeast of Puerto Rico. On September 16—just five days before the hurricane's landfall on Long Island—the SS *Algegrete* was rocked by a storm with winds in excess of seventy miles per hour. By September 19, hurricane warnings were posted for southern Florida, but the hurricane never struck there, instead taking a turn to the north.

At this time the weather bureau in Washington, D.C., started to monitor the storm's progress, but without modern technology like weather satellites, they greatly underestimated its northward speed and severely misjudged its track. Using the track that previous hurricanes had traveled, the weather bureau placed the hurricane farther out to sea with a more easterly heading, a path that would spare Long Island and New England. Two days later, on the morning of September 21, a Cunard liner close to the

Virginia coast recorded a very low barometric pressure of 27.85 inches. The strong cyclonic circulation of a hurricane creates low-pressure readings, and this reading suggested that the storm's path was much closer to land than the weather bureau had predicted.

For the previous one hundred years, hurricanes moving up the Atlantic seaboard had always deflected to the northeast, so the weather bureau held to its predicted path for the storm and posted only gale warnings from the mid-Atlantic states to coastal Maine, confident that the track would be well to the east of New England. With the approach of the storm, dramatic surf pounded the south shore of Long Island and the north shore of Long Island Sound, attracting thousands of beachgoers. Little was it known that a major hurricane, which had been building strength throughout the day, was going to hit land in synchrony with the seasonal equinox high tide.

By 3 PM on September 21, the weather bureau dramatically altered the projected storm path and predicted a landfall for Long Island and New England, but it was too late. The hurricane was already ravaging Long Island en route to southern New England. As a result of the low pressure in the storm's center, the ocean rose into a dome directly below the hurricane. Associated with the forceful pushing of the hurricane's southeasterly winds, a storm surge developed at landfall that was ten to seventeen feet above the autumnal high tide. This tidal surge swelled in a matter of minutes, sweeping away beach houses and onlookers alike both on Long Island and in coastal Rhode Island. The majority of the nearly seven hundred people killed by the 1938 hurricane perished in this storm surge.

The size of the hurricane—two hundred miles in diameter with an eye more than forty miles wide—made precise tracking of the storm center through New England difficult. The eye roughly followed the Connecticut River through southern New England and veered on a northwesterly diagonal through Vermont. By 5 PM the storm was centered close to Springfield, Massachusetts, and by 6 PM the eye passed over the south-central portion of Vermont's Green Mountains. Around 9 o'clock that evening, the storm's center exited Vermont near Burlington.

The stage for a major disaster had been set in the three days prior to the hurricane, when heavy rains dropped eight to eleven inches on southern and central New England. With an additional four to six inches of rain, much of it from dramatic cloudbursts dropped by the hurricane, the four-day totals ranged from twelve to seventeen inches. With the ground already saturated, the rain from the hurricane had nowhere to go but straight to the rivers.

The heaviest rains in central New England were concentrated in the Connecticut River watershed north to Hanover, New Hampshire. The Ashuelot, Deerfield, and Millers Rivers all set new flood-stage records by two to three feet, and the Merrimack equaled its previous record flood levels. In southern New England, all rivers set new records. The floods created havoc on bridges and towns alike, but it was the winds, in combination with the already saturated soils, that most impacted the region's forests.

The highest wind speed recorded during the hurricane was 186 miles per hour at the Blue Hill Weather Observatory near Boston, well to the east of the storm's center near the Connecticut River. As in all hurricanes, the strongest winds occurred on the eastern side of the storm, with sustained levels of over one hundred miles per hour near the southern New England coast and over sixty miles per hour in central New England. But it was the gusts of well over one hundred miles per hour that created the region's extensive blowdowns. Topographic settings such as ridgetops, slopes with southeasterly orientations, and gaps that funneled the wind were exposed to the strongest gusts and suffered the most severe blowdowns.

In New England, about a quarter million acres of forestland were leveled. It was estimated that three billion board feet of timber was downed. Much of it was never salvaged as the dramatic increase in sawlogs brought to the mills depressed market values, making most salvage operations uneconomical. In towns, churches lost their spires, and shaded, elm-lined streets became a maze of downed trunks through which cars wound their way single file. At the time, the Great Hurricane of 1938 became the most costly storm, in terms of property loss, ever experienced in the world. William Elliot Minsinger's book, *The 1938 Hurricane,* gives a wonderful written and photographic account of this historic storm.

Yet this was not the first, nor will it be the last, powerful hurricane to strike central New England. Since the landing of the Pilgrims, three other hurricanes have created extensive blowdowns in parts of New England's central region—in 1635, 1788, and 1815. The 1815 storm, known as the Great September Gale, was the record holder prior to 1938. (The center of this hurricane passed through Gardner, Massachusetts, and Jaffrey and Hillsboro, New Hampshire.)

Although hurricanes create widespread disturbance to central New England's forested landscape, their relative infrequency means that thunderstorms are responsible for the majority of the region's blowdowns. The July 15, 1995, thunderstorm heavily impacted 126,000 acres in New York State alone, about half the amount of forest damage created by the 1938 hurricane. Such a massive storm system is experienced in the Northeast only once in several decades, but smaller blowdowns resulting from thunderstorms are a frequent occurrence. The region's pillow-and-cradle topography is evidence of the prevalence of strong winds from the west. Yet of any single meteorological event, nothing can match the power of a well-developed hurricane to change the face of central New England's forested landscape.

chapter seven

TOPOGRAPHY AND SUBSTRATE

Through the first six chapters, our view of the forested landscape has been tightly focused. With the exception of beaver pond abandonment, all of the etchings place us in a particular forest setting. It is now time to step back and view the forested landscape at a larger scale. The preceding etching frames a river valley that runs north and south. From our vantage point, and from the level of detail rendered in the etching, it is difficult to discern the composition of the forests on the river's abutting hills. Based on the material we have covered thus far, do you think that the hillside forests to the right and left of the river are similar or different in their composition? You might have guessed that being on slopes facing different directions, one hillside forest may be more liable to fire or a blowdown than the other and therefore have a disturbance history that has created a forest of differing composition. This is good logic, and even if these forests share the same disturbance history, there are other reasons to believe that they are probably different. The reasons for these probable differences—*topography* and *substrate*—are the focus of this chapter. As we will see, there are a number of distinct forests in this river valley scene that are not clearly discernible in the etching, each associated with a specific substrate or topographic site.

The past six chapters have focused on the various phenomena that disturb and influence the shape of a forest. We have learned how to read signs of those disturbances so that we can reconstruct the history of a woodland. Interpretation of this kind is necessary because in most cases disturbance is the primary factor responsible for the structure and composition of our New England forests. However, topography and substrate also play critical roles in determining species composition on particular sites. To become more effective in reading the forested landscape, it is now necessary to shift our focus from the question "What happened here?" to a new question, "What kinds of plants and forests grow only in specific sites?" Together with disturbance, and the successional changes that follow it, topography and substrate are the sole forces that determine plant community composition in any phytogeographic region (with differing climates determining the placement of phytogeographic regions).

Topography relates to the lay of the land—the direction that slopes face and the steepness of their pitch. On sites with little slope, topography is not a factor. But where the land is pitched, many attributes of the site, particularly temperature and moisture, are profoundly influenced. Steep slopes and the crests of ridges with a southern orientation receive direct sunlight and are hotter and drier than other settings. Because they receive less sunlight, north-facing slopes and the sides of deep ravines are cool and moist. These conditions influence the composition of the species that are found in these different settings. In sites where topography creates extremes in temperature or moisture, we often find *eco-indicators*—species that have very specific requirements for their survival.

An eco-indicator's range of tolerance for particular factors—whether temperature, moisture, pH level, or a specific nutrient—is narrow, and eco-indicators grow only in sites where these factors meet their specific needs. Their presence automatically indicates attributes about the sites in which they are growing, thus the term eco-indicators. Many ferns are wonderful eco-indicators for soil moisture and nutrient levels. Bracken fern indicates dry, nutrient-poor soils, while sensitive fern grows only in wet, nutrient-rich soils. The elegant maidenhair fern indicates moist soils with high levels of calcium and a pH close to neutral. The presence of these species relays specific information about soil attributes that exert strong influences over forest composition. For example, when extensive patches of maidenhair fern are seen on the forest floor, a look to the canopy usually reveals bitternut hickory, white ash, and sugar maple. A knowledge of eco-indicators and the information they provide is necessary for interpreting forest composition. (Refer to the appendices for lists of both woody and nonwoody eco-indicators for central New England.)

MAIDENHAIR FERN

But it is possible to find specialized plants growing in sites with conditions far outside their tolerance range. The tamarack (also known as larch), North America's only deciduous conifer (it drops all of its needles in the fall), is a fine eco-indicator for moist to wet, acidic sites. It is most commonly found in acidic wetlands or on moist sands or gravels. But it is not uncommon to find it growing in parks, cemeteries, and lawns, sites that are usually neither wet nor acidic. If it is such a strong eco-indicator, how is it that tamaracks can grow in sites where moisture and pH levels are outside of their tolerance range? The answer can be found in what is known as the *germination niche*.

In biology, the term *niche* is often associated with animals, describing their ecological role in an ecosystem. In plant ecology, a niche is partially defined by the species' tolerance ranges, which are most narrow at the time of germination. Once successfully established, the tolerance ranges of plants expand. A tamarack can't germinate in a well-maintained lawn, but a young sapling can be successfully transplanted to one, so all the tamaracks we see in parks and yards are transplants. Because of the germination niche, an eco-indicator is useful to our reading of the landscape only when there is a robust population of that species. One or two individuals should not be used as indicators of site conditions, as their presence could be the result of some unusual chance events at the time of germination. These exceptions to the rule keep plant-community ecology from being an exact science, and they make the process of reading the landscape all the more interesting.

On the opposite side of the spectrum from the eco-indicators are the *generalists*—species of plants with very broad tolerance ranges for numerous factors. As a result, they can be found growing in just about any substrate or topographic site. Four very successful generalists in central New England are red maple, paper birch, white pine, and hemlock. They are ubiquitous in the region, and their presence usually tells us little about the topography or substrate of a specific area.

One of the reasons this book, and particularly this chapter, focuses on central New England and not a broader region is that the eco-indicator and generalist species found in one phytogeographic region are different from those found in another region. This is a particular problem for books that try to define the requirements for plants with broad ranges. The site requirements in one part of a plant's range are different from those in another part of the country. For example, white oak is a good indicator of warm, dry topographic sites in central New England, while in southern New England it is more representative of sites with moderate temperature and moisture levels. For specificity in reading the landscape, it is best to define eco-indicators within the context of a single phytogeographic region.

Other good indicators of warm, dry topographic sites in central New England are shagbark hickory, American chestnut, sassafras, and mountain laurel. Whenever forests with these species are encountered, it will most likely be on a site with southern exposure. Red oak and hop hornbeam are usually well represented on warm, dry sites, but because they also are commonly found in more moderate conditions, their presence doesn't necessarily indicate warmth and dryness. On the hottest and driest sites, chestnut oak, bear oak, and pitch pine will replace the species mentioned above.

Although the presence of an eco-indicator can be used to assess site conditions, its absence can't. As a number of the trees and shrubs mentioned above reach their northern range limits within central New England, they can be absent from large areas of the region. American chestnut, sassafras, mountain laurel, chestnut oak, and bear oak do not occur north of the lower portions of New Hampshire and Vermont. Balsam fir, a fine indicator of cool, moist sites, reaches its southern range limits in the region and is absent in north-central Massachusetts and southeastern New Hampshire.

Topography influences forest composition, but a much stronger impact on plants is generally exerted by *substrate*—the mineral material, such as clay, sand, gravel, glacial till, or bedrock, on which soil forms. Different substrates form a number of continua from wet to dry, fine grained to coarse grained, neutral and nutrient rich to acidic and nutrient poor. The association of pH to nutrient levels is related to important plant nutrients—primarily calcium and magnesium—being leached from acidic substrates and soils, so acidic soils are low in essential nutrients, while neutral soils are high in these nutrients.

Forest composition

Now that topography, substrate, and eco-indicators have been introduced, we can use them to interpret the forest composition of five different sites within the etching.

The first is a riparian site to the right or eastern side of the river. This site is dominated by floodplain forest, which lies at an extreme end of the substrate continuum. Floodwaters deposit alluvial silts and clays in these riparian sites, resulting in a fine-grained substrate that is rich in nutrients and very moist due to its low porosity. Because the substrate is fine grained, the pore spaces are very small, which means water can't percolate through it very quickly. Floodplain forests house a large number of site-specific eco-indicators, all of which are adapted to prolonged periods of flooding and the associated low levels of soil oxygen that flooding creates, but which also have high demands for nutrients. The canopy is usually dominated by silver maple, seen in the etching's lower right as trees gracefully arching over the river. The silver maple often bends like this, when growing close to a river, to gain more light. Sycamore—like the one to the left of the silver maples with its light, flaky bark—and eastern cottonwood—with deeply furrowed bark—are also common in New

SILVER MAPLE

England floodplain forests, along with American elm and hackberry. Box elder colonizes disturbed sites, and pure stands of five-foot-tall ostrich fern can carpet the forest floor. With the exception of the American elm, which can also occur in moist, rich upland forests, all these species are found only in floodplains.

These nutrient-rich floodplains, free of stones, are also the most productive agricultural lands in New England. The majority of these sites, like the field to the left of the river, now grow corn for dairy farms and comprise a large percentage of the nonforested land found in the region. Although botanists associate rich-sited woodlands with high levels of biodiversity, in riparian forests exposed to frequent flooding, plant biodiversity can be rather limited, with silver maple and ostrich fern—the region's two species of plants most tolerant of flooding—often creating monocultures. Yet the relationship between rich, productive sites and high levels of biodiversity is found on better-drained substrates where flooding and limited soil oxygen are not present.

OSTRICH FERN

Moving upslope from the floodplain forest we come to a west-facing hillside and find just such a site. Its soil is underlain by metamorphic rock with a high level of calcium. Calcium not only is an essential plant nutrient, but it also acts as a buffer to maintain a pH level close to neutral so other important nutrients are not leached from the soil. The slope keeps the substrate well drained while the fine texture of the soil keeps it moist. The forest growing on this site is a real treat for botanists, particularly in its rich composition of understory wildflowers and ferns.

Although they can't be distinguished in the etching, the trees that are the best eco-indicators for this kind of substrate are bitternut hickory and butternut. Associated with the hickory and butternut are other rich-sited trees, such as white ash, basswood, and American elm. The moderate-to-rich-sited sugar maple is also well represented. Maidenhair fern and blue cohosh are the classic understory specialists of these moist, neutral substrates, and a host of other herbaceous eco-indicators carpet the forest floor.

For the past twenty years, during the last week in April I have watched the weather reports hoping for a calm, overcast day. My schedule is organized to be free to spend such days, camera and tripod in hand, witnessing and recording the elegant wild-flower displays of rich, upland forests like the one I've just described. Shortly before the canopy leaves break bud, the vernal wildflowers of these sites are in their prime. I am greeted by the pink-striped petals of the spring beauty, the purple flowers of tril-lium, cohosh, and wild ginger (all colored to entice the first insects—carrion flies and beetles—to come out of winter dormancy), the bright yellow trout lily, the exquisite dutchman's breeches, and the earliest bloomer of them all, sharp-lobed hepatica.

I have recorded this last species blooming as early as March 26. Long before any other signs of spring in the plant world, hepatica sets forth its parabola-shaped flowers to track the sun. These flowers, ranging from white to pink to dark lavender, attract the very first flying insects. Slow-moving flies are drawn to the hepatica's tiny solar col-lectors, to warm themselves for further flight. Shortly after the hepatica comes into bloom, the sprouting of wild leeks creates lush green carpets that completely cover patches of the forest floor. By mid-April, before anything else has greened up, a walk in our rich-sited, upland forests will uncover spring proceeding at full speed. All of these herbaceous plants, along with butternut and bitternut hickory, are strong eco-indicators of moist, nutrient-rich upland soils, usually derived from bedrock substrates high in calcium.

As mentioned earlier, sugar maple is common in these rich forests, often dominating their canopies. Yet it is the presence of bitternut hickory and butternut that indicates the very rich, well-drained substrate, as sugar maple also grows well in sites with lower nutrient levels. Crossing the river to the hillside above the cornfield, on the left-hand side of the etching, is another forest dominated by sugar maple. The glacial till substrate under these maples also supports a good amount of beech, yellow birch, and black birch. All of these species grow well in moderate sites, sites that lie in the middle of the continua for moisture, temperature, pH, and nutrient levels.

With the exception of black birch, which is loyal to moderate sites in central New England, all the other trees found in the hillside forest I'm describing can grow in sites that veer away from moderation. Sugar maple does well in very rich sites, beech is successful in drier sites, and yellow birch moves into cooler, moister sites, often right into swamps. Thus, the relative abundance of these species can indicate attributes about their sites. If there is a good amount of beech, the site is probably a bit drier than moderate; if yellow birch is well represented, it is probably wetter.

Now let's leave this moderate-sited forest of beech, birch, and sugar maple and travel upslope to the exposed ledges on the southern end of the ridge (in the upper left corner of the etching). This site is extreme in terms of both topography and substrate. The resistant, granite bedrock holds little moisture; because of its mineral composition, it weathers into coarse, acidic, sandy substrates that collect in crevices and depressions. With the associated heat and dryness brought about by its steep southern exposure, this site is almost certainly fire-prone. Correspondingly, it supports the region's upland community that can most tolerate extreme heat, aridity, and lack of nutrients. The scraggly silhouettes of the widely spaced conifers growing on the ledges suggest an open forest of pitch pine, and although they can't be seen in the etching, bear oak and lowbush blueberry dominate the understory.

As discussed in chapter 1, pitch pine and bear oak, in association with white oak, are also commonly found on dry, sandy substrates where fire is frequent. Moister sand or gravel substrates, which have been recently disturbed through the removal of top-soil (a process common when excavating material from sandpits), most often support the growth of aspen, gray birch, paper birch, and white pine. These four species of small-seeded trees will colonize just about any site where disturbance creates litter-free conditions, so their presence is not restricted to sand or gravel. Yet if they are associated with the aromatic shrub sweetfern or the uncommon wildflower bristly sarsaparilla—both strong eco-indicators of sand and gravel—substrate determinations become easy.

Once again crossing the river to the ridgetop above the rich-sited forest, we find a site that is dry, but not to the degree of the southerly exposed granite ledges. It is dominated by red oak, a tree that does well on dry, wind-exposed ridges because its leathery leaves resist desiccation and its strong root system provides a solid anchor. In

SWEETFERN

each of the five sites we have examined in the etching—floodplain, rich hillside, moderate hillside, exposed granite ledges, and ridgetop—topography and substrate have created different conditions that have decidedly affected forest composition. Yet it isn't always possible to separate the influences of topography and substrate on a particular site, since topography can have a strong impact on substrate qualities.

The oak-dominated ridgetop, the exposed granite ledges, and the rich, well-drained hillside are examples of topography influencing substrate. In all these cases topography has a direct impact on the particle size, nutrient level, moisture level, and depth of the substrate, since water, dissolved nutrients, and fine materials are pulled downhill by gravity. Because of topography, the ridgetop and granite ledges have dry, nutrient-poor, coarse-grained substrates while the rich-sited hillside has just the opposite qualities. As with eco-indicators growing in unexpected sites, the influences of topography and substrate on the forested landscape are not always possible to neatly separate and interpret.

Sometimes the influences of topography and substrate are readily seen on a distant hillside or valley bottom; by looking at granite ledges like those in the etching, for example, we can immediately make some general assumptions about the forest we'd find there. But most of the time, like forest disturbance, the impact of topography or substrate will need to be read within a woodland setting, through the use of eco-indicators. To fully grasp the nature of our forests, learning to read the influences of disturbance, topography, and substrate is essential. The latter two are particularly important to a region like central New England, which is blessed with a rich variety of substrates and topographic sites. Sands, gravels, clays, silts, glacial tills, and bedrocks of various compositions are all found in a variety of topographic settings. This heterogeneity of the landscape in turn supports a diverse array of forest communities, but to decipher the differences among these many forest communities a knowledge of only three factors is needed: disturbance, topography, and substrate.

A LOOK BACK

Many geological events are responsible for central New England's diverse topography and substrates, but one stands out from the rest—the advance and retreat of the Laurentide Ice Sheet. Just eighteen thousand years ago, all of New England, a large portion of the northern Plains states, and all of Canada east of the Rocky Mountains were covered by an immense continental glacier. It marched south as far as Long Island and Nantucket, the depth of its ice in central New England reaching over five thousand feet. The formation of the Laurentide Ice Sheet and its sister continental glaciers in Eurasia dropped ocean levels worldwide by more than three hundred feet.

A glacier is formed when snow, compressed into ice, reaches depths of more than sixty meters. The sheer weight of this much frozen water crushes the precise molecular structure of the ice at the bottom of the glacier, forcing water molecules closer together. The result is that the ice is turned from a solid into a plastic. Plastic, I should say, is not just the stuff used to make so many of the products we use; it is also a state of matter, somewhere between solid and liquid. Plastics have form, but because their molecules are not locked into precise positions, plastics can change shape through the passage of time.

Anyone who has been in an old house has had direct experience with this process. The waviness in old windowpanes is the result of glass being a plastic. Under the pull of gravity, the molecules in the glass have slowly flowed from their original positions. The pull of gravity is also the force that causes glacial ice to move. As snow continues to build up on a glacier's surface, its weight forces the ice to flow laterally in a fashion similar to thick pancake batter being poured onto a griddle. Although the Laurentide Ice Sheet was born in Labrador, it eventually crept into New England through this process. As it flowed across the landscape, it created the bulk of the region's present topography.

Contrary to an image we might have of it, glacial ice is not clear and blue. Only near the glacier's surface is its ice free of contamination. In its depths the ice is loaded with particles of clay, silt, sand, gravel, and rocks of all sizes, picked up as the ice flowed over the land or actually quarried from the bedrock. With all of this embedded grit, the glacier acts as a huge sanding device with a power beyond our imagination, as it slowly—but completely—refinishes the surface of the landscape.

Throughout New England, glacial ice ground down through ecosystems, soil, and substrate. It then commenced on the bedrock, removing as little as a few feet from our most resistant granites to tens of feet from softer sedimentary and metamorphic rocks. Much of the region's bedrock, refinished by glacial sanding, still displays polished surfaces disrupted by scratches and gouges made by embedded rocks and boulders, respectively called *striations* and *grooves*.

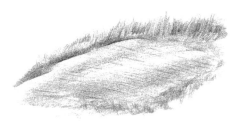

GLACIAL STRIATIONS

The ice sheet flowed through New England from north-northwest to south-southeast. Northwest-facing slopes and rock outcrops usually have gradual inclinations from the constant grinding of glacial ice, while southeastern faces are often steep, irregular ledges. On these faces the glacial ice lodged onto the bedrock and pulled out chunks as it passed southward. (Ledges quarried in this fashion are the origins for the region's many boulder trains mentioned in chapter 6.)

Most of the ridges and valleys in central New England are oriented north to south, the result of long-term glacial scouring. In some areas where glacial ice was forced through narrow valleys, the added pressure cut much farther into the bedrock, creating deep U-shaped ravines called *gulfs* or *notches*. All of the above features have been left in miniature on Rocky Ridge, a one-mile bushwhack from my house. A description of the ridge is worthwhile as it models on a small scale the pattern of the central New England landscape.

Rocky Ridge is the first ridgetop west of the Connecticut River in my town. It runs more or less north–south. Although the top is broad, it is anything but flat. Instead there is a series of parallel ledges of hard, glacially scoured schist, each ledge rising steeply anywhere from fifteen to fifty feet to a clean, rounded top.

In the narrow valleys between the ledges are either groves of old hemlock or acidic swamps dominated by winterberry holly and black gum. The black gum is considered rare in central New England, yet when I encounter a ridgetop swamp within a thirty-mile radius of my home, I often find this southern wetland species. It seems strange that a tree common in the Okefenokee Swamp of Georgia would inhabit such extreme, cold, nutrient-poor sites at the northern edge of its range. The black gum has been relegated to these ridgetops through competition with other New England swamp trees. On less extreme sites, black gum is easily outcompeted by red maple, black ash, hemlock, and yellow birch. However, in these tough, wind-exposed, ridgetop sites, our native swamp trees are more liable to windthrow than the black gum, which has lightweight, brittle wood. Winds that will topple maple, hemlock, birch, and ash usually remove only canopy branches from black gum, leaving the tree alive and standing.

On the ledge tops are outcrop communities dominated by reindeer lichen, haircap moss, lowbush blueberry, and black huckleberry, the exposed outcrops being the result of blowdowns and lightning-generated fires. The topography on Rocky Ridge is a microcosm for most of central New England, parallel north–south ridges with exposed bedrock tops separated by valleys housing wetlands and deep substrates. The advance of the ice sheet was responsible for developing this topographic pattern, and its retreat for creating the region's various substrates.

As previously mentioned, the maximum advance of the Laurentide Ice Sheet occurred eighteen thousand years ago. Following that time, the earth's global climate started to warm and the ice sheet began its retreat from New England. The rate of warming dramatically picked up about ten thousand years ago and initiated the *Holocene interglacial*—a warm period marked by the absence of North American and Eurasian continental glaciers. But New England didn't need to wait until the start of the interglacial to become ice-free; by fifteen thousand years ago the terminus of the ice sheet had retreated northward to central Connecticut, in another thousand years to northern Massachusetts, and finally by thirteen thousand years ago it had vacated all of New England with the exception of northern Maine.

Glacial deposits

It was the melting of the ice sheet, brought on by increasing global temperature, and the release of the glacier's mineral holdings that created New England's substrates. There were two categories of substrates created by the melting glacier: *stratified* and *unstratified*. Stratified substrates were created by meltwater ferrying materials away from the wasting ice and laying them down in horizontal layers. Clays and silts were carried into *pro-glacial lakes*—lakes that filled valleys exposed by the glacier's retreat and dammed by material dropped from the melting ice. The larger silt particles settled to the lake's bottom during the summer months, while the very fine clays remained suspended in the water until winter ice quelled wave action and cold temperatures reduced incoming stream flows. Today banded layers of clay and silt, known as *varved clays,* record not only where pro-glacial lakes existed, but also the variations in seasonal climates thousands of years ago, revealed by changes in the thickness of each band.

The three major pro-glacial lakes in New England were found at Lake Champlain and in the Merrimack and Connecticut River drainages. With a surface level seven hundred feet higher than today's Lake Champlain, Lake Vermont covered an area almost five times as great, giving rise to the rich agricultural lands of Vermont's Addison and Chittenden Counties. Lake Merrimack filled its valley from Concord to Franklin, New Hampshire. Lake Hitchcock covered 160 miles of the Connecticut

River valley from Rocky Hill, Connecticut, to Lyme, New Hampshire. All eventually broke through their dams of glaciar-deposited debris, draining thousands of square miles of former lake bed.

In shallow lakes with strong currents, streams with moderate currents, or at deltas where rivers flowed into larger pro-glacial lakes, sands were deposited by the meltwater. Sands created as the glacier ground down the White Mountains' hard granite were left as stratified outwash deposits in extensive areas of New Hampshire, southwestern Maine, and eastern Massachusetts. Outwash sands are not as common in Vermont and western Massachusetts, where the glaciation of the less resistant, metamorphic Green Mountains ground the bedrock to finer silts and clays. Finally, gravels were deposited by the fastest-flowing streams and rivers.

Any material that was dropped in place, without first being transported from the ice by meltwater, is said to be unstratified. The common term for jumbled unstratified substrate is *glacial till*. Till is a mixture of all particle sizes, from clays and silts up to rocks and boulders. Moving water never had the chance to sort the particles into different size classes. Tills can be highly variable mixtures and thus give rise to substrates with a wide range of qualities.

The distribution of stratified and unstratified substrates is strongly correlated to topography. Both our poorest, coarse-grained and richest, fine-grained substrates occur in the region's valleys, where, as glacial meltwaters slowed, they first dropped poor gravels and sands, and then rich silts and clays. In contrast, glacial tills are most commonly found on the slopes of ridges that frame the valleys, because meltwater never had the opportunity to transport these glacial deposits. Finally, tills dropped on ridgetops were often carried downslope by erosion, exposing the underlying scoured bedrock.

Return of life

With the region's substrates laid down by the glacier's retreat, New England awaited the northward march of vegetation that followed the withdrawal of the Laurentide Ice Sheet. By twelve thousand years ago, the central region was covered with sedge-dominated arctic tundra. This ecosystem housed the very last of many large Pleistocene mammals. It is thrilling to sit on a ridgetop, overlooking one of the region's valleys, and to think what we could see if we were transported back a mere few thousand years: grazing herds of woolly mammoths, giant bison, giant elk, and their most impressive predator, the short-faced bear, all roaming an open tundra landscape.

These, plus a few dozen other large mammals that existed prior to the Holocene interglacial throughout the northern hemisphere, have been named the Pleistocene megafauna. In all cases they were larger than modern-day counterparts. The Jefferson mammoth stood eleven feet at its shoulder, far taller than any modern elephant. The giant bison was 30 percent larger than any bison found in North America today. And the short-faced bear stood on legs that were six feet long. Our largest Kodiak bear, rearing up on its hind legs, would have had difficulty looking over the head of a short-faced bear standing on all fours. It's believed that the short-faced bear ran down its prey at speeds of forty-five miles per hour. There is no terrestrial predator in our modern world to compare with it.

Why were so many of these Pleistocene mammals so large? The species mentioned lived in tundra landscapes that bordered continental glaciers. These ecosystems were not only cold, but also subjected to sustained high winds generated by air circulation over the ice sheets. To survive in these climates, where wind-chill factors were extremely low, animals had to conserve heat by proportionately increasing the volume of their bodies with respect to their surface area; being large was the most effective way to stay warm.

All of the megafauna mentioned above, plus dozens of other species in the northern hemisphere, succumbed to a mass extinction about twelve thousand years ago. Many researchers suggest that these large mammals couldn't survive the fast-paced climatic changes brought about by the coming interglacial. Yet they had survived many similar interglacials during the previous two million years. Why would so many species in the northern hemisphere go extinct in this particular interglacial? Other researchers suggest that the difference during this most recent interglacial was the presence of a new species—*Homo sapiens.*

Modern humans, it is believed, evolved in Africa just prior to the previous interglacial, about one hundred thousand years ago. During the last glaciation, humans radiated throughout the world from Africa and were well established on all continents before the end of the Ice Age. It would have been hard enough for Pleistocene mammals to survive the rapid climate changes brought on by an interglacial because large mammals need extensive resources, and resources become limited in rapidly changing environments. With long gestation periods and low reproductive rates, such a change may have been too much when coupled with the introduction of the new super-predator, humans.

Interestingly, the *Pleistocene overkill,* as the extinction event is labeled by proponents of the theory that human hunting was its primary cause, occurred on all continents but Africa. This situation lends some support to the overkill theory because Africa was the only continent on which modern humans existed during the previous interglacial. Large African mammals that survived the presence of humans during the former interglacial would in all likelihood be able to repeat that feat during the Holocene. American and Eurasian megafauna, having never been exposed to human predation during a rapidly changing interglacial, would not be expected to fare as well. Africa is the only continent that continues to support vast herds of large mammals and represents what it must have been like in New England and the rest of North America just a few thousand years ago.

Luckily, not all large mammals were lost at the start of the Holocene. Musk oxen, caribou, and timber wolves were present in New England twelve thousand years ago, and as climates continued to warm and arctic ecosystems migrated northward, so did these surviving mammals. By ten thousand years ago central New England was covered in boreal—spruce and fir—forest. The most dramatic warming began nine thousand years ago, reaching its climax in 3500 BCE. This warmest time in the Holocene, called the *hypsithermal,* ushered in forests dominated by pines, oaks, and birches. Following the hypsithermal, world temperatures began a long cooling trend. It was during this period of cooling, approximately three thousand years ago, that the mixed forest we associate with present-day, central New England was finally established.

It is sobering to think that the forests we see as the hallmark of central New England have dominated the region for no more than 3 percent of the past one hundred thousand years. For the majority of that time, central New England was covered by arctic tundra or glacial ice. With respect to the Pleistocene's past two million years, what we know as the typical New England landscape is a dramatic anomaly. The "normal" New England during this period is much more like the Arctic region of Baffin Island, some fifteen hundred miles to the north.

chapter eight

FORESTS OF THE FUTURE

"Change is the only constant" is an adage well suited to the landscape of central New England. Whether wrought by human hands, storms, or longer-term alterations in climate, change has forged a dynamic landscape. As human observers who measure change in days and years, it is difficult for us to grasp that the landscapes we know in our lifetimes are not only ephemeral, but also often radically different from those that preceded them. In ways both predictable and unimaginable, the future landscape of central New England will differ from the one we know. In this chapter we will explore some possible phenomena that may impact the region's forested landscape in the future: forest fragmentation, declining forest health due to air pollution, and global climate change.

Only in the last decade has the number of people living in the rural portions of central New England begun to exceed the population level of 1840. As additional people choose to move to central New England, the region's forest will become more fragmented, reversing a 150-year trend of forest expansion through farm abandonment. Today when farms are sold, their open land is more likely to be developed than revert to forest. The vast majority of the region's remaining farmland is dedicated to dairy, a farm industry that has seen its subsidies cut; thus, the net loss of agricultural land will likely accelerate. Other specialty farm operations, like sheep farms and organic produce growers, will replace some of these retired dairies, but the bulk of the land will probably be lost to agriculture entirely since open land is highly sought for development.

But development does not only wait for abandoned agricultural land. In New Hampshire, more than twenty-one square miles of forest was converted to development in 1995 alone. As more people seek the quality of life offered by central New England, this trend is expected to continue. For the first time in more than a century, through the loss of farmland and woodland to development, central New England's forests are shrinking. At the same time, the region is experiencing an increase in the number of private landowners, which means that individual holdings are growing smaller as larger parcels are subdivided.

The combination of these factors—loss of agricultural land, conversion of forestland, and decreasing size of private land holdings—increases the fragmentation of the ecosystem and the potential for the loss of regional biodiversity. Fortunately, the creation of conservation land is also increasing in the region. Numerous land trusts, preservation trusts, forest societies, conservancies, towns, and individual landowners are setting aside large holdings that will be free from development and fragmentation. Even more hopeful is that many of these groups are working together to conserve contiguous parcels, creating large sanctuaries thousands of acres in size.

Meade Cadot, the director of the Harris Center in Hancock, New Hampshire, has been spearheading an effort to bring landowners together to create a "super-sanctuary" of over twenty thousand acres. He hopes to link eight thousand acres already protected in Hancock to a five-thousand-acre parcel in the adjoining town of Stoddard, owned by the Society for the Protection of New Hampshire's Forests and the Sweet Water Trust. Since the Stoddard property lies adjacent to the eleven-thousand-acre Andora Forest, Cadot's "super-sanctuary" is close to being a reality. In my town of Westminster, Vermont, the Windmill Hill–Pinnacle Association is working to link five hundred acres of ridgetop forest to other ridgetop conservation holdings in the towns of Putney and Dummerston in an attempt to create a single ridgetop preserve that could stretch over ten miles. On the slopes of Mount Equinox in Manchester, Vermont, the Equinox Preservation Trust has preserved over eight hundred acres of rich-sited forest and is working to link this with other parcels to create a preserve thousands of acres in size. All of these impressive projects have occurred in the last few years and, along with many other similar conservation efforts, are a necessary counterbalance to forest fragmentation brought about by development.

In light of these two opposing trends—fragmentation and conservation of central New England's woodlands—the region will remain predominantly covered by forest, but the landscape pattern will look different from how it does today. Large blocks of intact forest will be separated by increasingly fragmented forest holdings. Future vistas will show a landscape where forest patches will be more distinct than they currently are.

A second, potentially far more serious threat than the partitioning of the forest is the decline in regional forest health. In the past, forest health was defined by the concept of *sustained yield*—a forest that could grow wood products on a sustained basis was a healthy forest. More recently, the concept of forest well-being has expanded to include the health of the total ecosystem rather than just that of the canopy and understory trees. As mentioned in chapter 4, forest ecologists use three basic diagnostics to ascertain changes in ecosystem health: a decrease in the rate of photosynthesis within the ecosystem, an increase in the rate of nutrient loss from the ecosystem, and decreases in biodiversity over short periods of time. Declines in photosynthesis, nutrient holding capabilities, or biodiversity in short time frames that are not related to visible disturbance are all signs of ill health.

Certainly, as discussed in chapter 4, exotic blights have compromised forest health and remain a great threat to the region's woodlands. Yet during the past few decades, we have witnessed the decline of tree species where exotic pathogens may not be the sole cause. I stress "may not" because research on the decline of these species is far from complete. But if exotic diseases are not the primary cause, this may be the initial warning sign of a new problem that has the potential to be very serious: forest decline induced by air pollution.

In early May 1988, while driving back from a hiking trip in the White Mountains, I noticed that something looked different in the wooded hillsides traversed by Interstate 91. For the previous five years I had made this trip during the same week in May and knew that on my return the sugar maples of the Connecticut River valley would have broken bud, covering the hillsides in a first flush of green; this year, there was no green. When the maples broke bud, only tiny, yellowed, disfigured leaves appeared. I soon learned, as most Vermonters did, that during the previous month, the larvae of a small exotic insect from Europe—the pear thrips—had been feeding inside the buds of sugar maples throughout central and northern New England. In Vermont alone, a half million acres of forestland were completely defoliated.

The pear thrips, *Taeniothrips inconsequens,* is named for its usual association with fruit trees, but in the late 1970s it started to parasitize sugar maples. The expansion of the pear thrips' diet to include an entirely new tree species led some forest pathologists to speculate that our region's sugar maples may have already been weakened by other stressors and therefore were vulnerable to the pear thrips. When trees are weakened by environmental stressors, they are slower to mobilize their chemical defenses and become more liable to insect or fungal attack. Recent research on sugar maples has revealed that this tree species is indeed sensitive to numerous stressors, of both climatic and human origin.

CROWN DIEBACK

Sugar maples are more sensitive to drought, soil compaction, road salt, and atmospheric pollutants than just about any other common tree species in central New England. A casual examination of sugar maples growing along roadsides will usually show that they display more *crown dieback*—dead branches where healthy branches should be—than other species of trees. In roadside sugar maples the crown dieback is often the direct result of road salt. Since the 1980s, sugar maple decline has become a major concern to forest pathologists and is monitored annually by flyovers of established woodland plots by state foresters. In the 1994 aerial flyovers of Vermont monitoring sites, one out of twelve sugar maples suffered from serious crown dieback—serious meaning that more than 15 percent of the crown's branches were dead.

Atmospheric deposition

While crown dieback in sugar maples has numerous causes, including native insects, forest pathologists believe acid precipitation and other air pollutants play a role. Determining the strength of that role has been difficult because researchers have not been successful in isolating the impact of air pollutants from insect and fungal damage. As in sugar maple research, it was the synergistic interaction of numerous factors, and the associated inability to clarify the impact of any single factor, that eventually caused most of the Northeast's acid-rain research to be abandoned during the 1990s—no one could develop a direct link between acid precipitation and declining forest health. No one, that is, until Dr. Gene Likens and associate researchers working at the Hubbard Brook Experimental Forest in New Hampshire's White Mountains published groundbreaking research in an April 1996 issue of the journal *Science*.

What they discovered, after more than thirty years of data collection at Hubbard Brook, is that the forest basically stopped growing in 1987 and has been static ever since! Such a situation would be expected in an old-growth forest where trees have reached maximum size, but not in the much younger Hubbard Brook forest. More importantly, they were able to conclusively link the lack of forest growth to a loss of calcium and magnesium in the forest's soil—leached from the soil by acid precipitation. Two of the diagnostics used to ascertain the deteriorating health of an ecosystem directly apply to the Hubbard Brook forest: declining rates of photosynthesis and increasing rates of nutrient loss. The implications of this research—that forests in the Northeast may be experiencing growth stunted by acid precipitation—are unsettling.

But acid precipitation is only one aspect of a larger problem called *atmospheric deposition*—the fallout of numerous pollutants from the air. Not only acids fall from the sky; heavy metals, ozone, and organochlorines like DDT also rain out of the air. During the last half century the amount of new chemicals falling on our forests from the atmosphere has increased dramatically. Prior to World War II, about two dozen different chemical substances were known to occur in the lower levels of the atmosphere. Today, more than three thousand chemicals have been identified, the majority of which are new synthetic molecules created by humans. Recently, researchers in the White Mountains were shocked to find the organochlorine DDE, a by-product formed in the breakdown of DDT, in the bark of trees where DDT had never been applied. Further work confirmed that trees throughout New England have absorbed DDE, again in areas where DDT was never used. The origins of this atmospherically transported DDE are countries as far away as Asia, where use of DDT is not banned. While atmospheric pollution in the beginning of this century was a regional problem, it has become truly global at its close.

Sugar maple isn't the only tree showing signs of decline where the cause has not been directly linked to an introduced exotic pathogen. For the past thirty years the butternut has been dying throughout its range, and the decline has been so dramatic that this species may become the first North American tree to be listed as a rare and endangered species. The cause of the decline is a fungus—butternut canker—whose Latin name, *Sirococcus clavigignenta-juglandacearum,* is every bit as large as its impact on its host. First detected in Wisconsin in 1967, this fungus of unknown origin has now spread throughout the northeastern quarter of the United States and bordering Canada. In New England the majority of butternut are standing dead snags, and fewer than one out of five remaining live trees is considered healthy. This blight has all the signs of an introduced exotic, and numerous researchers believe it is, but the fungus has not been identified elsewhere in the world. The question comes to mind, If it is not an exotic, but instead a native fungus, why has it become so lethal in the last thirty years? Could it be that butternuts have been weakened by environmental stress, allowing the fungus to become virulent? At this point, there is no answer to the origins of the butternut blight, nor any cure.

Another tree experiencing a decline in recent decades is white ash. Like the butternut, it has a newly identified pathogen called an MLO (mycoplasma-like organism). MLOs are primitive single-celled organisms but, unlike their relatives the bacteria, they do not have a cell wall. The MLO that attacks white ash grows in the tree's vascular tissue causing a condition known as "ash yellows," in which the canopy dies back. The beginning of ash yellows can be noticed by reduced vigor in the crown, with leaves growing in tufts at the end of twigs. This tufting is caused by slowed growth rates in the twigs, so that the nodes where the leaves grow become packed together at its terminus. But ash yellows are only part of the problem in the decline of this tree in central New England. Many ash showing canopy dieback are not infected by the MLO, just as numerous ash that have the MLO appear healthy with no sign of canopy decline. Like the sugar maple, white ash is a species sensitive to many environmental stressors. In those areas where there is greater stress, the lethal effects of ash yellows are more pronounced. It may be that the MLO associated with white ash normally exhibits a very mild form of parasitism, and only when the tree is weakened by other factors does the relationship change to one of a lethal nature.

For the past decade, I have suspected that canopy dieback similar to that in ashes has been occurring in red oak. In a number of areas that I frequent, I have observed thinning in red oak canopies brought about by leaf tufting and twig dieback. Recently I established study plots in the towns of Keene, Chesterfield, and Hinsdale, New Hampshire, to monitor red oak canopy coverage, but I do not yet have data to back my casual observations. At present, regional forest pathologists are not seriously concerned about canopy decline in red oak because trees with thinning crowns continue to grow well as leaves once shaded gain full sunlight, but I believe this is a species that should be more closely watched as another indicator of changing forest health.

With the possible exception of the butternut, the above species—sugar maple, white ash, and red oak—have all developed canopy decline as a result of a number of factors rather than a single introduced pathogen. Perhaps these trees could be compared to the canaries used in mine shafts to monitor air quality. Because all have developed problems fairly recently, they may be the first indicators that humans have created too many stressors for forest ecosystems in New England: changes in land use, introduction of exotic species, changes in community composition, and, most recently, constant exposure to air pollutants, to name a few.

At present we are seeing crown dieback only in certain species of trees, and, luckily, not in whole forests. In areas of eastern Europe, where there has been no regulation of air pollution during the past half century, huge expanses of both coniferous and broad-leaved forest have been lost. Large portions of Germany's famed Black Forest have experienced forest decline where two out of every three trees have died. Although other factors, such as the removal of downed wood—an important source of soil nutrients—to maintain a parklike appearance, have also influenced the declining health of these forests, atmospheric deposition has played the chief role.

Recently there has been debate at the federal level to roll back portions of the Clean Air Act. The proposed changes to weaken the act would result in increases in atmospheric acids, heavy metals, PCBs, and ozone. I am convinced that, eventually, this would also mean greater canopy decline in New England forests. Luckily, the American public is overwhelmingly in favor of protective environmental legislation, so the Clean Air Act should remain intact. But we need to do more than just maintain the status quo. We need to further reduce atmospheric pollutants, and our success in doing so will be reflected in healthier forest ecosystems.

Global warming

Often associated with atmospheric pollution is the process of global warming. There is no doubt that the earth's climate is getting hotter. The warmest year ever recorded (since the mid-nineteenth century, when mean global temperatures were first monitored) was 1995, with an average annual temperature of 59.7 degrees Fahrenheit. This topped the previous record holder—1990. A single-year record could be an anomaly, but looking at five-year increments since the 1970s shows that each succeeding five-year period has gotten warmer.

Associated with this warming has been a dramatic melting of alpine glaciers and portions of the Antarctic Ice Sheet. Alpine glaciers around the world have lost 10 percent of their ice in the latter half of this century. In March 1995, a thousand-square-mile chunk of Antarctica's Larsen Ice Shelf broke away to melt at sea. In New England, as in the rest of the world, regional climates have become more dramatic and erratic. Weather patterns became so fast paced during the spring of 1996 that many New England weather forecasters joked about their inability to predict the next day's weather. Due to losses from ever more powerful storms during the 1990s, insurance companies became the largest private funding source for global warming research.

Although there is no doubt that the earth's climate is heating up, the question remains: Is human activity the major cause of global warming? The vast majority of climate-change researchers believe that human activity—particularly carbon dioxide released through the combustion of fossil fuels—*is* the primary cause. In 1995, the Intergovernmental Panel on Climate Change—an organization of twenty-five hundred climate-change researchers worldwide—issued a finding that states that human activity is responsible for global warming, and unless serious steps are taken to reduce emissions of carbon dioxide, the heating of the earth will be the most serious environmental problem of the twenty-first century.

What are the implications of global warming for New England's forested landscape? To address this question, we first need to examine how the New England countryside responded to a previous trend in global warming—the transition from the last glaciation to the Holocene interglacial. As mentioned in chapter 7, the Laurentide Ice Sheet made its maximum advance in the Northeast eighteen thousand years ago; this point in time also marks the coldest mean annual global temperature of the last ice age: 51 degrees Fahrenheit. Then the earth's climate started to warm and ten thousand years ago we entered the Holocene interglacial. Global temperatures continued to increase until the hypsithermal peak fifty-five hundred years ago, with a mean global temperature of 60 degrees Fahrenheit. To appreciate the implications for our present global warming trend, we need to note that it took more than twelve thousand years for the average global temperature to rise nine degrees, from the coldest to the warmest temperatures the earth has experienced in the last one hundred thousand years.

During this warming trend and following the glacier's departure thirteen thousand years ago, wave after wave of plants migrated into central New England as climates warmed. The rate of speed with which these plants could extend their northward ranges was controlled by two factors: the age at which an individual plant produced seeds and the means by which it dispersed its seeds. Trees that, at a fairly young age, produced small, windblown seeds that could disperse long distances—like aspens, birches, and conifers—migrated more quickly than any other kind of tree, expanding their range northward at rates of up to a mile every three to four years. Trees that took longer to reach reproductive age and produced large nuts dispersed by animals, like chestnuts and hickories, were the slowest migrants, requiring an average of sixteen years to move a mile northward. The key point is that the rate at which a tree can adjust its range is directly related to its reproductive strategy.

Supercomputer modeling during the past decade has consistently predicted that mean global temperature will rise another four degrees Fahrenheit by the middle of the twenty-first century if we do nothing to curb emissions of carbon dioxide. With the warming that has already occurred during the past fifty years, this means that the earth will warm 4.5 degrees in the period of one century. When we compare this rate of change to the nine-degree rise that took twelve thousand years during the transition from glacial to interglacial, it is sixty times faster! How will tree species adjust their ranges to climates changing at such a fast rate? If the warming is as dramatic as predicted, trees won't be able to match its pace, resulting in broad-scale disruption of forest communities.

For central New England, the models predict that the warming will be most obvious during the winters, which will become milder and wetter. Summers will be slightly hotter and drier. The result will be a climate more similar to that of Maryland. For species of trees that don't grow south of New England (or do so only at high elevations), such as red pine, larch, balsam fir, red spruce, quaking aspen, paper birch, yellow birch, and pin cherry, the warming climate will most likely translate into an inability to germinate successfully. These species of trees would decline in the region's forests. If summers become hotter and drier, drought-sensitive trees like sugar maple and white ash will experience more dieback from the increased environmental stress. At the same time, southern trees that could thrive in New England's warming climate, like sweet gum, sourwood, post oak, chinkapin oak, and loblolly pine, will take centuries to complete a northern migration to the region. The obvious result would be a dramatic reduction in the variety of tree species that compose central New England's forest.

But the impact won't be restricted to the obvious. New England trees with ranges that do extend far to the south, such as red oak, hemlock, black cherry, and black birch to name a few, may have problems that we can't foresee because of the rapid rate of climate change. Certainly trees won't be the only organisms affected. Many plants, animals, and fungi will be impacted in ways that are hard to predict. The one certainty is that if this unprecedented global warming occurs, central New England will see noticeable reductions in biodiversity. Coupling these reductions with those already created by introduced forest pathogens and potential declines from atmospheric deposition, we see a very bleak picture of our future forests.

There is a Mohawk prophecy relating to canopy dieback in sugar maples that says when the tops of the maples are seen to be dying, it will be a sign of great change to come. Well, the tops of the sugar maples *are* dying, and we find ourselves poised at the start of a century that could be typified by dramatic reductions in forest health. But there is also another, much more hopeful interpretation of this prophecy: Possibly the "great change" will finally be a global effort to right our environmental wrongs.

It is not hard to be pessimistic about our environmental future, but it is also not hard to be optimistic. In the last thirty years, the world's population has moved from an almost complete lack of awareness of its impact on the earth to an understanding that humans are affecting global ecology. In the next decade or two, our knowledge of global warming and atmospheric deposition should be far more solid than it is today. When we have clear knowledge about the cause of environmental problems, we nearly always take steps to correct them—the worldwide ban on the production of CFCs (chlorofluorohydrocarbons) to save the ozone layer being a good example. We have the knowledge, technology, and the resources to clean up our environmental messes—we need only the willpower. That willpower is fostered in two ways: by an understanding of our environmental problems, which we continue to gain, and through the wisdom to see that we are inescapably dependent on and intrinsically connected to the natural world.

I am an ecologist today, and have written this book, because I discovered my connection to the land through the woods of my childhood. Now when I wander through the forests and fields that surround my home, I am not just a tourist passing through, but a part of the landscape—a partner in its dialogue. Through this relationship I continue to gain respect and reverence for the land, its history, its changes, and its well-being. It is this kind of relationship that I deeply believe needs to be fostered more widely in our human community. Although this book is a guide to reading the history of New England's forests, it also has another, possibly less obvious, role. It is an invitation, an opening, to a deeper relationship with the land, a relationship that, as it grows, will, I hope, foster environmental advocacy. I am optimistic about the long-term well-being of our forested landscape because I believe we continue to gain greater understanding and wisdom. It is my hope that *Reading the Forested Landscape* will play a part in that process.

A CENTRAL NEW ENGLAND CHRONOLOGY

18,000 BCE	Laurentide Ice Sheet reaches maximum expansion; coldest temperatures of the last glaciation
15,000 BCE	Laurentide Ice Sheet retreats northward to central Connecticut
14,000 BCE	Laurentide Ice Sheet continues its northward retreat to northern Massachusetts
13,000 BCE	Laurentide Ice Sheet retreats from all of New England with the exception of northern Maine
12,000 BCE	Arctic tundra covers central New England; evidence of first human presence in New England; start of mass extinction of Pleistocene megafauna
10,000 BCE	Start of Holocene interglacial; boreal spruce and fir forest dominates central New England
9000 BCE	Dramatic warming ushers in forests dominated by pines, oaks, and birches
5500 BCE	Hypsithermal peak, warmest temperatures during the Holocene; earliest archaeological evidence of Native use of fire for landscape management in central New England

Note: *BCE means before the common era*

1000 BCE	Forests of present composition dominate central New England
1000 AD	Maize agriculture adopted by New England Natives, which in association with fire creates coastal prairies and riverine intervales
1524	Giovanni da Verrazano explores the New England coastline
1616	The first major epidemic, possibly chicken pox, kills 95 percent of coastal New England Natives
1636	William Pynchon establishes a fur-trading post in Springfield, Massachusetts; trapping of beaver and other furbearers by Natives for British trade escalates dramatically
1654	The first recorded cutting of "mast pine" for the British navy
1675	The first battles between the Algonquin tribes of central and northern New England and the British commence eighty-five years of sporadic warfare for control of the region; the Algonquins are backed by the French
1691	Dwindling supplies of mast pine lead to the marking of trees with the "broad arrow" in an attempt to keep colonists from cutting them
1760	The French defeat at Montreal brings the end to Native warfare with the British; the dramatic migration of British settlement into central New England begins
1810	Following Napoleon's victory over Portugal, William Jarvis imports four thousand merino sheep to Vermont and starts thirty years of "sheep fever"; the beaver is extinct from central New England
1815	The Great September Gale
1825	The Erie Canal opens access to the rich Ohio River valley
1840	The sheep industry and rural population levels peak in central New England; farm abandonment and a mass migration to the Ohio River valley and parts west begin

1860	The introduction of the gypsy moth to Massachusetts for silk production research and the moth's escape into New England's forests
1890	The accidental introduction of beech bark scale disease to Nova Scotia
1900	Resurgence of white pine, on abandoned pastures, as the region's most important timber species; the development of the sustainable yield concept in American forestry
1904	The accidental introduction of the chestnut blight into New York
1921	The first reintroduction of beaver into central New England
1930	The first American elms start to die in Ohio due to Dutch elm disease
1938	The Great Hurricane
1988	Pear thrips defoliate five hundred thousand acres of Vermont's forest, initiating new canopy-decline research in New England
1990s	Human populations in rural central New England towns grow to what they were in 1840
1995	A global warming trend that began in the middle of the nineteenth century pushes global temperatures close to those of the hypsithermal; the mean global temperature is the warmest ever recorded

A READING PRIMER

In this book, as in the classes I teach, I use examples of forests with distinct and easily observable disturbance histories. This is necessary to give people the foundation needed to read the landscape. Yet I must caution that many forests do not display the distinct disturbance patterns I have described because their histories are blurred by many separate events—often numerous logging operations on top of previous disturbances. But do not despair if first attempts at reading forested landscapes are frustrating. It's the process of attempting to read forest histories that's important, not necessarily finding the correct interpretation. The process will generate questions, and the questions become the real teachers in this exercise, forcing us to look for repeated patterns and to stretch observational and analytic skills. It took numerous visits to sites impacted by fire, for example, before I realized that age discontinuities are a classic sign of this form of disturbance.

To begin the process of reading the landscape, look for changes in forest composition or age. Is the difference of one site from another due to a shift in topography or a change in substrate? Look for eco-indicators that might confirm the influence of one or both of these factors. If the change in forest composition involves generalists, differing disturbance histories are most likely at work. As I have done in the first six chapters, start looking for evidence of the six common forms of forest disturbance in New England: fire, pasturing, logging, blights, beaver, and blowdowns. But most important, have fun as you work to unravel the stories inscribed in your local woodlands.

EVIDENCE OF FORMER DISTURBANCE

FIRE

Standing dead snags
Conifers and oaks made rot resistant by heat-killing that stand for many decades; often silvery in appearance.

Discontinuity in age classes
Fires often leave the overstory and create a vigorous understory, but will usually remove the midstory trees. Logging will not do this; age discontinuity can be observed only in forests with trees more than two feet in diameter.

Basal fire scars
Triangular scars at the base of trees, on the uphill sides if on a slope. This is where fuel pockets form. If the trees are not on a slope, the scars will be randomly distributed wherever fuel pockets occurred.

Multiple-trunked trees
Many broad-leaved trees and pitch pine send up stump-sprouts after they have been heat-killed.

Charcoal
After ten years, charcoal is not very visible unless you dig in the soil, and even then it may not be found. Also, certain fungi that grow on decaying sugar maple and beech look very much like charcoal but are not, so fire should always be verified by means other than charcoal alone.

PASTURING

Stone walls
Constructed with large stones; the presence of many fist-sized stones indicates past cultivation.

Barbed wire
Barbed wire was first used in the early 1870s. Its presence indicates pastures that were used in the last century.

Wolf trees
Wide, low-branching trees, originally left when woods were cleared to shade animals.

Thorny shrubs
Hawthorns, barberry, and roses all deter browsing.

Juniper
A slow-growing, unpalatable shrub that is released by the grazing of grass that would otherwise overtop it. The only other environments in which it is common are on rock outcrops and in poor coarse soils where herbaceous vegetation is not able to overtop it in its early years of growth.

Weird apples
Apple trees that are highly contorted at their base and often have many basal branches near the ground; a result of heavy browsing pressure.

LOGGING

Multiple-trunked trees
Many broad-leaved trees send up stump-sprouts after they have been cut.

Cut stumps
Stumps that have a visible flat top.

Opposing basal scars
The skidding of logs damages the bases of trees on skidder roads, creating basal scars that face one another and are often triangular in shape.

Softwood stumps
Decay from the outside in.

Rot-resistant hardwood stumps
Decay from the inside out.

BLIGHTS

Snags with fungus
Trees killed by blights (insect or fungal) are not rot resistant and quickly develop fungi. The exceptions to this are the American chestnut and oaks—all are naturally rot resistant.

BEAVER ACTIVITY

Standing dead snags in water
Flooding kills trees, but the anaerobic conditions created by the flooding preserve the root systems, allowing dead snags to remain standing for decades. These trees are usually conifers and birches—low-preference species.

Beaver-cut stumps
Blond-colored stumps indicate beaver activity within the year; gray stumps were cut more than a year ago; stumps with turkey tail fungi growing on them were cut at least three years ago.

Beaver dams
The first sign of beaver abandonment is a drop in water level below the top of the dam. Herbaceous vegetation growing on the pond side of the dam indicates abandonment at least two months previously. Woody vegetation growing on the pond side indicates abandonment of at least two years.

BLOWDOWNS

Downed trees
Trees all lying in the same direction. Downed trees lying in all directions indicate that dead trees fell over at various times.

Pillow-and-cradle topography
When a live tree is blown over, its upended roots carry a lot of earth, creating a depression, or "cradle." When the tree and root system rot, the earth is dropped as a pile, or "pillow," next to the cradle. Pillow-and-cradle topography lasts for hundreds of years.

Decayed nurse logs
Most often hemlock trees growing in a line with exposed roots tracing the line.

SITE CONDITIONS FOR COMMON WOODY PLANTS OF CENTRAL NEW ENGLAND

alder, speckled (Alnus rugosa)
moderate to rich wetlands

ash, black (Fraxinus nigra)*
rich swamps

ash, green (Fraxinus pennsylvanica)*
rich, alluvial sites

ash, white (Fraxinus americana)
rich, moist sites

aspen, bigtooth (Populus grandidentata)
moderate sites

aspen, quaking (Populus tremuloides)
generalist; strong on coarse, dry substrates

arrowwood, northern (Viburnum recognitum)
moderate to rich wetlands

barberry, Japanese (Berberis thunbergii)
pastures

basswood, American (Tilia americana)*
rich, moist sites

beech, American (Fagus grandifolia)
moderate to dry sites

birch, black (Betula lenta)
moderate sites

birch, gray (Betula populifolia)
generalist; strong on coarse, dry substrates

birch, paper (Betula papyrifera)
generalist

birch, yellow (Betula lutea)
moderate to moist, cool sites

blueberry, highbush (Vaccinium corymbosum)*
acidic uplands and wetlands

blueberry, lowbush (Vaccinium angustifolium)*
acidic, dry sites

Note: * *signifies strong eco-indicator*

buckthorn, European (Rhamnus frangula)
generalist

butternut (Juglans cinerea)*
rich, moist sites

cedar, eastern red (Juniperus virginiana)*
warm fields

cherry, black (Prunus serotina)
rich, moist or poor, dry sites

cherry, pin (Prunus pensylvanica)
generalist

chestnut, American (Castanea dentata)*
warm, dry sites

cottonwood, eastern (Populus deltoides)*
alluvial sites

dogwood, alternate-leaf (Cornus alternifolia)
moderate sites

dogwood, red-osier (Cornus stolonifera)
moderate to rich wetlands

dogwood, silky (Cornus amomum)
moderate wetlands

elderberry, common (Sambucus canadensis)*
rich, wet sites

elderberry, red (Sambucus pubens)
moderate to poor sites

elm, American (Ulmus americana)*
rich, moist sites

elm, slippery (Ulmus rubra)
moderate to rich sites

fir, balsam (Abies balsamea)*
moist, cool sites

hawthorn (Crataegus sp.)*
pastures

hemlock, eastern (Tsuga canadensis)
generalist

hickory, bitternut (Carya cordiformis)*
rich, moist sites

hickory, shagbark (Carya ovata)*
rich, warm sites

hobblebush (Viburnun alnifolium)*
cool sites

hop hornbeam (Ostrya viriginiana)
rich, dry sites

huckleberry, black (Gaylussacia baccata)*
dry, poor, burned sites

ivy, poison (Toxicodendron radicans)
rich, moist or poor, dry sites

juniper, common (Juniperus communis)*
pastures, rock outcrops, or poor, coarse
substrates

laurel, mountain (Kalmia latifolia)*
acidic, warm sites

laurel, sheep (Kalmia angustifolia)*
acidic uplands and wetlands

leatherleaf (Chamaedaphne calyculata)*
acidic wetlands

locust, black (Robinia pseudo-acacia)
rich sites

maple, ashleaf (Acer negundo)*
alluvial sites

maple, mountain (Acer spicatum)*
cool sites

maple, red (Acer rubrum)
generalist

maple, silver (Acer saccharinum)*
rich, alluvial sites

maple, sugar (Acer saccharum)
moderate to rich sites

musclewood (Carpinus caroliniana)*
rich, moist sites

nannyberry (Viburnum lentago)*
rich wetlands

oak, chestnut (Quercus prinus)*
hot, dry sites

oak, red (Quercus rubra)
moderate to warm, dry sites

oak, white (Quercus alba)*
warm, dry sites

oak, scrub (Quercus ilicifolia)*
poor, dry, burned sites

pine, pitch (Pinus rigida)*
poor, dry, burned sites

pine, red (Pinus resinosa)*
poor, dry, ledgy sites

pine, white (Pinus strobus)
generalist

sassafras (Sassafras albidum)*
warm, dry sites

spicebush (Lindera benzoin)*
rich wetlands

spruce, black (Picea mariana)*
acidic wetlands

spruce, red (Picea rubens)*
acidic, cool sites

spruce, white (Picea glauca)*
northern valleys

sweetfern (Comptonia peregrina)*
poor, coarse substrates

sycamore (Plantanus occidentalis)*
rich, alluvial sites

tamarack (Larix laricina)*
acidic, wet sites

viburnum, mapleleaf (Viburnum acerifolium)*
acidic, dry sites

Virginia creeper (Parthenocissus quinquefolia)*
rich, moist sites

witch hazel (Hamamelis virginiana)
warm sites

wild raisin (Viburnum cassinoides)*
acidic wetlands and uplands

COMMON NONWOODY ECO-INDICATORS
FOR CENTRAL NEW ENGLAND

bloodroot (Sanguinaria canadensis)
rich, wet sites

blue cohosh (Caulophyllum thalictroides)
rich, moist sites

bracken fern (Pteridium aquilinum)
poor, dry sites

bristly sarsaparilla (Aralia hispida)
poor, coarse, dry substrates

bunchberry (Cornus canadensis)
acidic, cool sites

Canada lily (Lilium canadense)
rich, moist, often alluvial sites

Canada mayflower (Maianthemum canadense)
acidic, dry sites

checkerberry (Gaultheria procumbens)
acidic, dry sites

cinnamon fern (Osmunda cinnamomea)
acidic wetlands

clintonia (Clintonia borealis)
acidic, cool sites

false hellebore (Veratrum viride)
rich, wet, alluvial sites

goldthread (Coptis groenlandica)
acidic, cool sites

haircap moss (Polytrichum juniperinum)
coarse, dry or bedrock substrates

hay-scented fern (Dennstaedtia punctilobula)
moderate to poor sites

Jack-in-the-pulpit (Arisaema atrorubens)
rich, moist sites

jewelweed (Impatiens capensis)
rich, wet sites

maidenhair fern (Adiantum pedatum)
rich, moist sites

miterwort (Mitella diphylla)
rich, moist sites

ostrich fern (Matteuccia struthiopteris)
rich, alluvial sites

painted trillium (Trillium undulatum)
acidic, cool sites

partridgeberry (Mitchella repens)
acidic, dry sites

pink lady's slipper (Cypripedium acaule)
acidic uplands

red baneberry (Actaea rubra)
rich, moist sites

red columbine (Aquilegia canadensis)
rich, dry sites

red trillium (Trillium erectum)
rich, moist sites

royal fern (Osmunda regalis)
moderate wetlands

sensitive fern (Onoclea sensibilis)
rich wetlands

sharp-lobed hepatica (Hepatica acutiloba)
rich uplands

skunk cabbage (Symplocarpus foetidus)
rich, warm, swamps

spring beauty (Claytonia virginiana)
rich, moist sites

starflower (Trientalis borealis)
acidic uplands

trailing arbutus (Epigaea repens)
acidic, dry sites

trout lily (Erythronium americanum)
rich, moist sites

wild ginger (Asarum canadense)
rich uplands

wild leek (Allium tricoccum)
rich, moist sites

GLOSSARY

adventitious bud   A bud found on roots and trunks of trees.

age discontinuity   A gap in the age classes of trees in a forest.

Algonquin Nation   The tribes of New England and eastern Canada that shared the same linguistic heritage.

Ascomycetes   A class of mostly inconspicuous fungi that produce spores in a saclike cell called an *ascus*.

atmospheric deposition   The deposition of air pollutants through dry fall and precipitation.

basal rosette   A growth form in herbaceous plants where all the leaves radiate from the top of a rootstock and lie flat on the ground.

basal scar   A wound at the base of a tree's trunk where the bark has been removed by fire or some form of collision.

beaver meadow   An abandoned beaver pond that is vegetated by sedges and rushes.

beech snap   The breaking of a beech tree's trunk following infection by beech bark scale disease.

biomass   The total amount of living and dead organic matter in an ecosystem.

blowdown	The toppling of living trees by strong winds.
boulder train	Boulders transported by a glacier from a particular point of origin and deposited in a path across the countryside.
cambium	The thin layer of living tissue of a tree that lies just beneath the bark.
canopy decline	The thinning of a forest's canopy due to leaf loss from pathogens or stress.
commensalism	An interrelationship between individuals of different species in which one of the individuals benefits while the other remains unaffected by the interaction.
coppice	Trees with more than one trunk growing from their root system; multiple trunked.
Cowasuck	An Algonquin tribe of the upper Connecticut River valley.
crown dieback	The loss of a tree's living branches from pathogens or stress.
deadfall	The toppling of dead trees following root system decay.
disturbance	A disruption to an ecosystem's successional progression resulting in a new ecosystem that has lower rates of photosynthesis and less ability to hold nutrients.
eco-indicator	A plant with very specific requirements for moisture, temperature, or nutrients.
epiphyte	A plant that grows on trees.
forest composition	The species of trees and other plants present in a forest.
forest decline	The death of trees in a forest due to pathogens or stress.
forest structure	The sizes and spatial distribution of a forest's trees.
frass	Caterpillar excrement.

frost crack	A vertical crack in a tree's trunk caused by the rapid contraction of its bark.
fuel pocket	An accumulation of forest litter or woody material at the base of a tree.
generalist	A plant that can grow under a wide variety of conditions; the opposite of an eco-indicator.
germination niche	The specific, often narrow requirements for the successful germination of a plant's seed.
girdling	The killing of the cambial tissues all the way around a tree's trunk, eventually resulting in the death of the root system.
glacial till	The mineral material directly dropped by a retreating glacier without being transported and stratified by meltwater.
heartwood	The central wood of a tree's trunk that doesn't transport sap.
heat-killing	The girdling of a tree from the heat of a fire.
Holocene	The geological time period of the past ten thousand years typified by interglacial conditions.
hummock	A mound, produced by the roots of trees, that rises above the water table in swamps.
hypsithermal	The warmest period of the Holocene interglacial, 3500 BCE.
intervale	A riparian grassland created by years of Native agriculture and burning.
Laurentide Ice Sheet	The last continental glacier to cover New England, the Northern Plains states, and Canada east of the Rocky Mountains.
leader	The vertical, topmost branch on a coniferous tree; the terminal shoot.
mast	Nuts and large seeds produced by trees.
mast year	The production of an unusually large amount of seeds by a species of tree in a given year.

merino	A Portuguese breed of sheep that produces a high quality fleece.
Missisquoi	An Algonquin tribe of the eastern shores of Lake Champlain.
MLO	A mycoplasma-like organism, similar to a bacterium but without a cell wall.
multiple trunked	Trees with more than one trunk growing from their root system; coppiced.
mycelium	The unseen bulk of a fungus that is within decaying wood or the soil and is composed of fungal *hyphae,* or threads.
nurse log	A decaying log, usually a conifer, in which trees successfully germinate and grow.
nurse shrub	An unpalatable or thorny shrub of pastures that shields young trees from browsing livestock.
Pennacock	An Algonquin tribe of the Merrimack River valley.
permaculture	Agricultural systems that produce a variety of crops without annual planting.
phytogeographic region	An area that shares the same climate and supports the same mix of vegetation.
Pigwacket	An Algonquin tribe of the Saco River valley.
pillow-and-cradle topography	Pits and mounds resulting from a blowdown.
pit-and-mound topography	See pillow-and-cradle topography.
plant community	An aggregation of plant species interacting in an ecosystem.
Pleistocene	The geological time period of the past two million years characterized by repeated and extensive global glaciation.

Pleistocene overkill	The theory that human hunting was responsible in part for the extinction of dozens of large mammals twelve thousand years ago.
pro-glacial lake	A lake that formed at the front of a retreating glacier.
riparian	Relating to the floodplains, banks, and terraces that line rivers.
sapwood	The outer wood of a tree's trunk that transports sap.
sheep fever	The central New England sheep-farming craze that occurred between 1810 and 1840.
skidding	The dragging of cut trees out of a forest.
Sokoki	An Algonquin tribe of the middle Connecticut River valley.
snag	A standing dead tree.
stratified substrate	Glacial outwash transported and deposited by meltwater.
stylet	The tubular, sucking mouthpart of a sap-eating insect.
substrate	The mineral material on which soil forms.
succession	The changes in plant communities following a disturbance resulting in increasing rates of photosynthesis and the ability to hold nutrients; ecosystem maturation.
sustained yield	The forest management concept of being able to harvest forest products on a continual basis.
tannin	A plant toxin that makes proteins indigestible.
terminal shoot	The vertical, topmost branch on a coniferous tree; the leader.
thunderstorm microburst	A powerful downward gust of wind generated in severe thunderstorms.
topography	The lay of the land, the steepness and direction of its slopes.

unstratified substrate	The mineral material directly dropped by a retreating glacier without being transported and stratified by meltwater; glacial till.
varved clays	Bands of silt and clay deposited in the bottoms of pro-glacial lakes.
wampum	Colored cylindrical beads fashioned from the shells of whelks and quahogs.
Western Abenaki	An affiliation of the Cowasuck, Missisquoi, Pennacook, Pigwacket, and Sokoki tribes.
whorled	Branches radially arranged around a point in a tree's trunk.
wolf tree	An open-grown, wide-spreading tree, so named because it often stands alone in a forest of younger trees.

SELECTED BIBLIOGRAPHY

INTRODUCTION

Jorgensen, Neil. *A Sierra Club Naturalist's Guide to Southern New England*. San Francisco: Sierra Club Books, 1978.

Marchand, Peter J. *North Woods*. Boston: Appalachian Mountain Club, 1987.

Watts, May T. *Reading the Landscape*. New York: The Macmillan Co., 1964.

chapter one
THE AGE DISCONTINUITY

Bromley, S.W. *The Original Forest Types of Southern New England*. Ecological Monographs, 1935. 5:61–89.

Cronon, William. *Changes in the Land: Indians, Colonists, and the Ecology of New England*. New York: Hill and Wang, 1983.

Day, Gordon M. The Indian as an Ecological Factor in the Northeastern Forest. *Ecology*: (1953) 34:329–346.

Gordon, Whitney. *From Coastal Wilderness to Fruited Plain: A History of Environmental Change in Temperate North America 1500–Present*. Cambridge: Cambridge University Press, 1994.

Patterson, William A., and Kenneth E. Sassaman. *Indian Fires in the Prehistory of New England: Holocene Human Ecology in Northeastern North America*. George P. Nicholas, ed. (New York: Plenum Publishing, 1988) pp. 107–135.

Russel, Emily W. B. Indian-Set Fires in the Forests of the Northeastern United States. *Ecology:* (1983) 64:78–88.

chapter two
OF JUNIPERS AND WEIRD APPLES

Allport, Susan. *Sermons in Stone: The Stone Walls of New England and New York*. New York: W. W. Norton & Co., Inc. 1990.

Calloway, Colin G. *The Western Abenakis of Vermont, 1600–1800: War, Migration, and the Survival of Indian People*. Norman: University of Oklahoma Press, 1990.

Cronon, William. *Changes in the Land: Indians, Colonists, and the Ecology of New England*. New York: Hill and Wang, 1983.

Foster, David. Land-Use History (1730–1990) and Vegetation Dynamics in Central New England. *Journal of Ecology:* (1992) 80:753–772.

Gordon, Whitney. *From Coastal Wilderness to Fruited Plain: A History of Environmental Change in Temperate North America 1500–Present*. Cambridge: Cambridge University Press, 1994.

Heffernan, Nancy C., and A.P. Stecker. *New Hampshire: Crosscurrents in its Development*. Grantham, NH: Thompson and Rutter Inc., 1986.

Holden, Raymond P. *The Merrimack*. New York: Rinehart & Co., 1958.

Ludlum, David M. *Social Ferment in Vermont 1791–1850*. New York: Columbia University Press, 1939.

Thompson, Betty F. *The Changing Face of New England*. New York: The Macmillan Co., 1958.

Wikoff, Jerold. *The Upper Valley: An Illustrated Tour along the Connecticut River Before the Twentieth Century*. White River Junction, VT: Chelsea Green Publishing Co., 1985.

chapter three
A STUDY IN STUMPS

Foster, David. 1992. Land-Use History (1730–1990) and Vegetation Dynamics in Central New England. *Journal of Ecology:* (1996) 80:753–772.

Gordon, Whitney. *From Coastal Wilderness to Fruited Plain: A History of Environmental Change in Temperate North America 1500–Present.* Cambridge: Cambridge University Press, 1994

Hawes, Austin P. New England Forests in Retrospect. *Journal of Forestry:* (1923) 21:215.

Pike, Robert E. *Tall Trees, Tough Men.* New York: W.W. Norton & Co., Inc, 1984.

chapter four
NECTRIA

Baldwin, Ian, and Jack Schultz. Rapid Changes in Leaf Chemistry Induced by Damage: Evidence of Communication Between Plants. *Science:* (1983) 221:277–279.

Houston, David R. Beech Bark Disease: The Aftermath Forests Are Structured for a New Outbreak. *Journal of Forestry:* (1975) 73:660–663.

Little, Charles E. *The Dying of the Trees: The Pandemic in America's Forests.* New York: Viking, 1995.

chapter six
PILLOWS AND CRADLES

Foster, David R., and Emery R. Boose. Patterns of Forest Damage Resulting from Catastrophic Wind in Central New England. *Journal of Ecology:* (1992) 80:79–98.

Jorgensen, Neil. *A Sierra Club Naturalist's Guide to Southern New England.* San Francisco: Sierra Club Books, 1978.

Oliver, Chadwick D., and Earl P. Stevens. Reconstruction of a Mixed-Species Forest in Central New England. *Ecology:* (1977) 58:562–572.

Minsinger, William E. *The 1938 Hurricane: An Historical and Pictorial Summary.* Boston: Blue Hill Observatory, 1988.

chapter seven
TOPOGRAPHY AND SUBSTRATE

Davis, Margaret B. Holocene Vegetational History of the Eastern United States. *Late Quaternary Environments of the United States.* H.E. Wright, ed. (Minneapolis: University of Minnesota Press, 1983) pp. 166–81.

Fowells, H.A. *Silvics of Forest Trees of the United States.* Washington, D.C.: US Department of Agriculture, 1965.

Jorgensen, Neil. *A Guide to New England's Landscape.* Old Saybrook, CT: The Globe Pequot Press, 1977.

Kurten, B. *Before the Indians.* New York: Columbia University Press, 1988.

Pielou, E.C. *After the Ice Age: The Return of Life to Glaciated North America.* Chicago: University of Chicago Press, 1991.

Raymo, Chet, and Maureen E. Raymo. *Written in Stone: A Geological History of the Northeastern United States.* Old Saybrook, CT: The Globe Pequot Press, 1989.

Ruddiman, W.F., and H.E. Wright Jr. *The Geology of North America: North America and Adjacent Oceans During the Last Deglaciation.* vol. K–3. Boulder, CO: The Geologic Society of America, 1987.

chapter eight
FORESTS OF THE FUTURE

Likens, Gene E., et al. Long-Term Effects of Acid Rain: Response and Recovery of a Forest Ecosystem. *Science:* (1996) 272:244–246.

Little, Charles E. *The Dying of the Trees: The Pandemic in America's Forests.* New York: Viking, 1995.

Peters, R.L., and T.E. Lovejoy. *Global Warming and Biological Diversity.* New Haven: Yale University Press, 1992.

Ruddiman, W.F., and H.E. Wright Jr. *The Geology of North America: North America and Adjacent Oceans During the Last Deglaciation.* vol. K–3. Boulder, CO: The Geologic Society of America, 1987.

INDEX

BIOGRAPHIES

Tom Wessels is an ecologist whose teaching for the past twenty years has focused on the landscape of central New England. He is the associate chair of the Environmental Studies Department at Antioch New England Graduate School, where he directs the Environmental Biology Program. He lives with his wife, Marcia, and daughter, Kelsey, in the hand-hewn log house they built in Westminster, Vermont.

Brian D. Cohen is a printmaker, artist, and teacher who was chair of the Putney School Art Department from 1985 to 1994, when he founded Bridge Press, located in Saxtons River, Vermont. His etchings and fine edition letterpress books are in the collections of Dartmouth College, Harvard University, Mills College Center for the Book, the Portland Museum of Art, Smith College, Stanford University, and the University of Vermont.